Life how short, Eternity how long

Gravestone Carving and Carvers in Nova Scotia

Life how short, Eternity how long

Gravestone Carving and Carvers in Nova Scotia

Deborah E. Trask

The Nova Scotia Museum
Halifax, N.S.
1978

Published by
The Nova Scotia Museum
as a part of
The Education Resource Services Program
of the
Department of Education
Province of Nova Scotia

Hon. Terence R. B. Donahoe
Minister

Carmen F. Moir
Deputy Minister

ISBN 0-919680-09-7 (cloth.)
ISBN 0-919680-12-7 (paperback.)
© The Nova Scotia Museum 1978

Printed in Canada

Produced by the
Nova Scotia Communications and
Information Centre, Box 2206
Halifax, N.S. B3J 3C4
1978

Contents

All photographs by Deborah Trask
unless otherwise noted.

The First Cut:
A Very Brief and General
History of a Gravestone
Tradition

Gravestones as functional objects were not new when the first Europeans came to North America. This method of marking the burial sites of human remains had been evolving for hundreds of years within western culture.

We should perhaps begin with the idea of burial as tradition. Interment appears to have been practiced long before recorded history as the simplest and most natural way of disposal. Beyond this is the ancient belief that man was first formed out of earth and should best go back when the time comes to leave. This belief was well entrenched by the time the Book of Genesis was written. ". . . till thou return unto the ground; for out of it wast thou taken: for dust thou art, and unto dust shalt thou return" (Genesis 3:19).

The custom of marking the spot is closely tied to the fact that people have never been able to accept death as an ending. In the classical areas of the Mediterranean are found effigies, painted or in stone, of the deceased as they appeared in life. Stone, as a natural object, was used for commemoration, and the belief evolved that stones became the spiritual residences or even counterparts of the dead.[1] Stone symbolizes something eternal.

The first areas set aside specifically for the inhumation of the dead were outside of city walls and unconnected with churches. Over time, however, the burial sites of holy people became themselves shrines. Eventually churches were built over them. Early Christian churches felt it was important to house holy relics in the altar.[2] Naturally everyone of consequence wanted to be buried as close to the relics as possible, as if insuring (by osmosis) a foot in the door of heaven. Remains are to be found packed into the walls and floors of medieval churches, and spewing out into the yard. This privilege was at first limited to ecclesiastics, then royalty, but quickly deteriorated to whoever could pay the most.[3] With the Protestant Reformation this trend abated somewhat, particularly in North America where "purer" theology did not include the worship of holy relics. But custom is hard to break, and graveyards continued to have church affiliations. This was because burial rites were, and are, still considered as religious ritual and because the church, central to the community, was often used for secular activities as well. Stone, though its use evolved in a pre-Christian tradition, continued to commemorate the dead, sometimes carved to depict a moral lesson for the living, and later to show effigies of the souls of the deceased.[4]

In Nova Scotia the first burial grounds were also in central locations, usually near fortifications and churches; and with the geographical spread of a population without focus, family burial areas were located on private land. Wherever located, something was left to mark the spot and, more importantly, to commemorate the deceased. Whether humble or elaborate, these markers remain static decorative objects — fixed in time and in space — among the earliest examples of indigenous creative art.

French and Indians

The native peoples of Nova Scotia (Micmacs), although they also practiced inhumation, appear not to have used decorative markers for graves as did the Haida in British Columbia, for instance.[1] There is recorded the following description of a Micmac burial in inland Queens County about 1860:

. . . he landed there one afternoon with his father and mother and younger brother, who was taken sick in the night and before morning was gone forever. The next day his father made a grave and fashioned a bark coffin, and the dead child was pillowed on moss, the grave covered with flat stones, and left to the care of Him who marks the sparrow's fall . . . a ring of smooth, pretty pebbles from the beach encircled the grave.[2]

At Kejimkujik National Park (between Annapolis and Liverpool) there were a number of supposedly Micmac gravestones, now destroyed, which were really field stones set on end, occasionally engraved with a simple cross or date (Fig. 1).

It is possible that the French settlers also used rough fieldstone grave markers, but more probable that they used wooden crosses. These were perhaps destroyed by the surging hordes of post-expulsion Protestant immigrants in their haste to take over Acadian lands; more likely, such crosses simply rotted over time.[3] In any case, I can find no evidence of distinctive early Acadian art in grave markers.

Figure 2
Bathiah Douglass, Annapolis Royal,
Annapolis Co.; slate, 1720.

Figure 3
Rebecca Douglass, Annapolis Royal,
Annapolis Co.; slate, 1740. No
longer standing.
(Photo by William Inglis Morse)

Figure 4
Lettice Doane, Barrington,
Shelburne Co.; slate, 1766.

2

Imported Stones of the Eighteenth Century

3

4

Gravestone history in Nova Scotia begins really after 1714 with the nucleus of a Protestant (mainly British) population. Mainland Nova Scotia became one of the new English outposts in North America following the Treaty of Utrecht in that year, and immediately thereafter English military people moved into the only fortified settlement — renaming it Annapolis Royal for the just-dead English Queen, Anne. This remained the political and military centre of Nova Scotia for thirty-five years until the founding of Halifax.

It is not surprising therefore that the oldest English gravestone in Canada is to be found at Annapolis Royal. This is the Bathiah Douglass stone (Fig. 2) and is elaborately carved slate, probably made around Boston.[1] The image is of a toothy winged skull, usually called a death head. Notice the swirled border. The Bathiah Douglass stone is in mint condition. The stone of her successor in the Douglass household has not fared as well (Fig. 3).

This fascinating slate stone, undoubtedly carved in New England, is known only from a photograph, taken by William Inglis Morse before 1932. Death is depicted as a simple incised skeleton holding a sickle and leaning on an hourglass, deciding who he is going to cut down next. The stone was also at Annapolis Royal.

Death heads were very popular in seventeenth and early eighteenth century New England gravestone fashion. Curiously, there are very few found in Nova Scotia, and all of these appear to have been imported. The Lettice Doane stone (Fig. 4) is typical. The Mary Hilton stone (slate, Chebogue, 1774), another standard death head, is signed "Abraham Codner Next the Drawbridge Boston" (Fig. 6). Many imported death heads are in the Town Point Burying Ground, Chebogue, Yarmouth County, with a few in Halifax, Annapolis Royal, Truro, Liverpool, Port Medway and Barrington. What is interesting is that these are not found in *all* the areas of pre-Loyalist settlement. There are no death heads in the Chester, Londonderry, Onslow, Amherst, Newport, Falmouth, Horton or

5

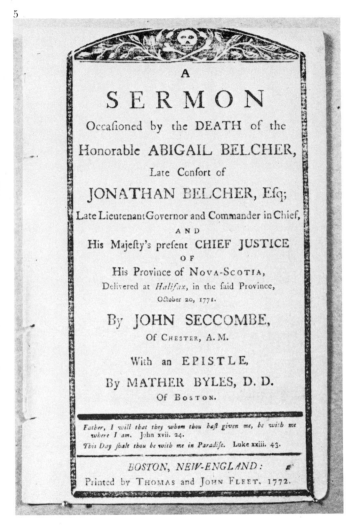

6a

6b

Figure 7
Margaretta Newton, St. Paul's
Cemetery, Halifax; slate, 1769.

Figure 8
Stephen Collins, Liverpool, Queens
Co.; slate, 1793. Signed: "L. Maxcy
Sc. Salem Massachusetts".

Figure 9
John Crowninshield, Salem,
Massachusetts; slate, 1777.

7

8

9

Cornwallis regions. Another interesting point is that this was old fashioned in New England gravestone taste by the time of the American Revolution and yet several imported stones from the 1770's and 1780's, in Chebogue and Liverpool in particular, show standard death heads.

There is a theory in the study of demographic history, "the immobility of fragmentation"[2] which states simply that when a group of people move away from the society they have known to start a new society, they lose, for a time, the stimulus toward change that the old society provided. They therefore remain stagnant, fixed with the ideas in vogue at the time of their departure. As New England had been a fragment of England, so Nova Scotia from 1760 was a fragment of New England. This theory of fragmentation and resulting traditionalism is made tangibly visible in gravestone taste in Nova Scotia. The people of Liverpool and Chebogue, even though they were sending to the Boston area for their stones anyway and could have had the latest design, chose instead to purchase what had been to them a traditional gravestone design when they lived in that area.

More common than death heads are soul effigies, or cherubim.[3] In Liverpool, Chebogue and Halifax are many beautifully carved cherubim on slate from the Boston area. The Margaretta Newton stone (slate, 1769) (Fig. 7) for example, was obviously imported — possibly carved by William Codner in Boston.[4] In Liverpool, the Stephen Collins stone (slate, 1793). (Fig. 8) is signed "L. Maxcy, Sc. Salem Massachusetts". This is not a portrait of Mr. Collins as there are several exactly like this in Salem (Fig. 9). The Benajah Collins stone (slate, 1788) (Fig. 10), also at Liverpool, was probably carved by Maxcy as well.

Figure 10
Benajah Collins, Liverpool, Queens Co.; slate, 1788.

Figure 11
Dan Webster, Chipman's Corner, Kings Co.; sandstone, 1785. Signed: "Chester Kimball N. London".

10

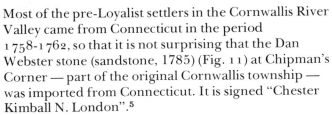

11

Most of the pre-Loyalist settlers in the Cornwallis River Valley came from Connecticut in the period 1758-1762, so that it is not surprising that the Dan Webster stone (sandstone, 1785) (Fig. 11) at Chipman's Corner — part of the original Cornwallis township — was imported from Connecticut. It is signed "Chester Kimball N. London".[5]

Angel Heads

By far the greatest number of early nineteenth century decorated gravestones (before 1800 to about 1830) show winged heads, or soul effigies. The change in religious thought that led to this transition in death imagery, from graphic symbols of mortality to symbols of resurrection, is complex, confusing and beyond the scope of this study.[1]

More interesting is the source. Where did gravestone image-makers get the idea of using a winged head to symbolize the departed soul? Why not a winged heart? In the Bible, angels serve mainly as messengers, and their only connection with death is to convey the elect soul into the presence of God, or some nice place. See, for example, the parable of the rich man and Lazarus (Luke 16:22), "And it came to pass that the beggar died, and was carried by the angels into Abraham's bosom; the rich man also died, and was buried". In Calvinist thought, death did not mean instant elevation to the ranks of angels, not even for a true believer.

Dr. Ludwig has attempted to explain the presence of angel images as a blend of guardian angels, glorified souls becoming angelic bodies, and created angels performing their proper duties in bearing the soul to heaven.[2] This is a reasonable assumption, taken from contemporary literary sources.

However, we must remember that pictorial sources were very limited in the eighteenth century and before. What kinds of visual imagery were popularly available? I don't pretend to know. Dr. Ludwig mentions that stonecarvers in New England used broadsides, engravings, woodcuts, book plates and illustrated primers for their borrowings.[3] Emblem books which developed as a pictorial-literary genre in sixteenth century Italy became popular throughout western Europe in the seventeenth century. These served as pattern books for decorative artists and engravers. In England, the *Emblemes* of Frances Quarles, printed in 1635, had a widespread distribution. The illustrations were taken from earlier popular Jesuit emblem books.

Dr. Ludwig has already proved Quarles' *Hieroglyphikes* (1638) to have been the source for an elaborate stone in Boston dated 1678.[4] It is possible that the winged angel head has its source in this type of popular publication that was distributed in North America. See, for example, an emblem of George Wither[5] (Fig. 12), which shows a winged figure clutching a cross, with one foot on a skull and the other on an hourglass, fixing his eye on heaven. "Where er'e we dwell, the Heav'ns are neere; let us but fly, and wee are there."

I think the idea of the guardian angel is the most credible. There is a Biblical source for this in Psalm 91, verses 11 and 12:

For he shall give his angels charge over thee,
to keep thee in all thy ways.

They shall bear thee up in their hands, lest thee
dash thy foot against a stone.

This theme was expanded by Quarles in Hierogliph V:[6]

You blessed Angels . . . will you be pleas'd to . . .
guard the dust that lies before yee?

Whatever the source, angel heads or cherubim became the single most popular gravestone image. This image arrived in Nova Scotia from New England as a fashion in gravestone carving. I doubt that the carvers themselves were much concerned about the source of this image.

There is much more room for individual interpretation in carving angel faces (which are still in the realm of the imagination) than death heads — a skull is a skull.[7] By the late eighteenth century the first local carvers were working in Nova Scotia. If they used imagery at all, they used the angel head — perhaps to signify the departed soul, perhaps the guardian angel. The cherub had become a customary gravestone image.

Figure 12
"Where er'e we dwell, the Heav'ns are neere; Let us but fly, and wee are there."
Emblem of George Wither, 1635
(Book 3 illustration XVIII) (Photo by R. Merrick)

Where er'e we dwell, the Heav'ns are neere;
Let us but fly, and wee are there.

ILLVSTR. XVIII.   Book. 3

Primitive Local Carving

Figure 13
Graveyard, east side, Sable River, Shelburne Co. Fieldstone grave markers in foreground.

Figure 14
Black Brook Cemetery, Port Morien/Mira, Cape Breton Co. Fieldstone grave markers in foreground.

Figure 15
Jannet McDonald, Hacketts Cove, Halifax Co.; slate, 1789/1791.

13

14

15

By the period of the American Revolution rural Nova Scotians had advanced beyond subsistence level and started to produce things for themselves — perhaps someone in the community could afford to take the time to chisel out a stone. With the Revolution, the importation of gravestones from New England virtually ceased. This is not to say that all grave markers dating from before the Revolution had come from New England. In Halifax, which was somewhat more settled, carvers like James Hay (see Hay Family) were working. Also some stones appear to have come from England. In a great many coastal areas the people remained so poor or so scattered that no markers were used at all. This is especially true around the Eastern Shore and parts of Cape Breton.[1] On Cape Sable Island and in several burial grounds along the Sable River, graves were marked by pieces of field stone set on end (Figs. 13, 14). It is impossible to determine when this was done, but it was probably a common practice in isolated areas.

At Hacketts Cove on St. Margaret's Bay, Halifax County, stands a stone commemorating several members of the McDonald family, c. 1791[2] (Fig. 15). This is a nicely carved piece of slate. The imagery consists of a simple cross over IHS,[3] indicating that the family was Roman Catholic. Although the decorative details are not sufficiently interesting to catch your eye, the bottom part of the script states: "This stone is Erected by Hugh McDonald . . .& is the first Stone Erected in St. Margaret Bay." This may imply that earlier gravemarkers were of wood. What it says, with considerable pride, is that this is the first actual gravestone — not just any old piece of fieldstone.

The Horton Carver
(c. 1783-1793)

Fifteen to twenty years after the first English-speaking settlers arrived in the area of the Basin of Minas, a person in the township of Horton began to carve gravestones for his neighbours. His identity has yet to be revealed, but in the old burial grounds around Wolfville are many examples of his work. The Horton carver, working in sandstone, used simple incised lines, and his stones are rich in symbols. This says something about the literacy level in late eighteenth century Nova Scotia, as well. The mass of population could not read. The Major Thomas Leonard stone in Wolfville (sandstone, 1783) (Fig. 17) is one such stone. The carver has used, basically, three lines to depict a cherub.

Under the cherub are crossed bones, meaning the mortal body, and above the cherub is a spiked crown, representing the resurrected soul. There is also a crude hand, presumably death, holding a sickle, ready to cut down anyone; and an upright hourglass to show any passers-by foolish enough to look at it that the sands of time were running out for them too. The symbols are there to point out the moral lesson of death to all those good people who could not read. The cherub head itself is so simple it could also mean the sun, symbolically setting on Major Thomas Leonard's life, to rise again, hopefully, in heaven.

In each base corner of the elder Elizabeth DeWolf stone (Fig. 19) (Wolfville, sandstone, 1784) stands a wiggly tree, with an axe laid across it. This may signify the lopping off of the tree of life by an unseen hand. What is interesting is that in Nova Scotia this image is unique to the Horton-Cornwallis region, where many of the early settlers came from Connecticut.

In the area of Truro and Onslow are a number of sandstone gravestones carved obviously by the same hand, depicting images very similar to the Horton sun-cherub, although not as well cut. These date from 1774 to 1793. Most of the people they commemorate were related to the Archibald clan and came from the North of Ireland via Londonderry, New Hampshire, to Truro in about 1762.

16

Figure 17
Major Thomas Leonard, Wolfville,
Kings Co.; sandstone, 1783.

Figure 18
Elizabeth DeWolf, Wolfville, Kings
Co.; sandstone, 1783.

Figure 19
Elizabeth DeWolf, Wolfville, Kings
Co.; sandstone, 1784.

Figure 20
Eloner Archibald, Truro, Colchester
Co.; sandstone, 1781.

17

18

19

20

The Second Horton Carver (1798-1805)

Figure 21
Joseph Chase, Junior, Upper
Canard, Kings Co.; sandstone,
1798.

There appears to have been another carver working in the Horton-Cornwallis area shortly after the Horton carver, also working exclusively in sandstone. This carver may have possibly been two people, but I think it more likely that he merely changed his style after a few years.

In the first period (1798-1801) he carved sad cherubim with deep outlines around the face. See the Joseph Chase, Junior stone (Upper Canard, Kings Co., sandstone, 1798) (Fig. 21)[1]. The rope edge and bird track border are the same in both periods. The shaping of the top is a simple curve at first. In the second period (1801-1805) the top shape became more elaborate, with the addition of a bracket around "Here Lies" and further cutting away around the head — perhaps to show a halo. See, for instance, the Martha Harris stone (Upper Canard, Kings Co., sandstone, 1802)[2] (Fig. 23).

The base of the Lucretia Rogers stone (Wolfville, Kings Co., sandstone, 1801) (Fig. 25) shows a coffin shape with a very simple, tiny head and crossed arms inside. The carver appears to have used a printed model for his letters — notice particularly the "g" in Age. For an unskilled person it is much easier to carve straight lines in stone, as the Romans did.

21

Figure 22
Benjamin Peck, Kentville, Kings
Co.; sandstone, 1801

Figure 23
Martha Harris, Upper Canard,
Kings Co.; sandstone, 1802.

Figure 24
Eunice Harris, Upper Canard,
Kings Co.; sandstone, 1803.

Figure 25
Lucretia Rogers, Wolfville, Kings
Co.; sandstone, 1801.

22

24

23

25

The Annapolis Carver

On the assumption that a number of stones in one area obviously carved by one person must have been made in that area, I should like to be able to attribute many of the old stones of Annapolis County to an Annapolis carver. This is not a valid assumption, however. The Old Loyalist Burying Ground in Saint John, New Brunswick, contains a large number of stones which appear to have been carved by the same person who made those in Annapolis. As Saint John, in the period 1800-1820, was a considerably more booming metropolis than Annapolis, it seems probable that the Annapolis carver actually worked out of Saint John.[1]

Working in sandstone, the Annapolis carver preferred the image of a winged cherub. There is one example of his work in Shelburne, one in Yarmouth, several in Clementsport, Annapolis Royal and all along the Annapolis River. See, for example, the Benjamin McConnell stone (sandstone, 1808) (Fig. 26) in North Weymouth, Digby County. A distinctive characteristic of the Annapolis carver is in the shape of the stone, which tapers to a small but high curve at the top. Thus the wings always look cramped.

It is interesting to compare the work of the Annapolis carver with that of his contemporary, Abraham Seaman (see Seaman family).

26

28

27

29

German Stones

Figure 30
*Ana Catheriena Zwicker, Mahone
Bay, Lunenburg Co.; slate, 1780.*

Figure 31
*Johan George Eisenhauer, Mahone
Bay, Lunenburg Co.; slate, 1805.*

Early nineteenth century German stones are to be found in Lunenburg, Mahone Bay and Chester as well as in scattered areas along the coast in Lunenburg County. These stones are generally of slate, roughly quarried and very crudely carved with simple hearts or plants.

The earliest are in German; for example, the Ana Catheriena Zwicker stone, Mahone Bay, which is slate, dated 1780 (Fig. 30). There are no poems, scriptural references or witty epitaphs found on German stones. The lettering is often crude capitals or curious gothic script. Spacing between words is erratic. Sometimes only a dot indicates the end of a word, and whenever a line was filled, words were split and carried over into the next.[1]

The Johan George Eisenhauer stone (Mahone Bay, Lunenburg Co., slate, 1805) (Fig. 31) is decorated with a very Germanic dancing tulip — similar to "Pennsylvania Dutch" motifs. The text, in gothic script, reads:

30

*Hier Ruhet Johan Ge
orge Eisenhauer. Ist ge
bohren zu Wilhelms
feld in Teutschl, ANNO
1733 22d Jan. Kömt nach NO
VA SCOTIA 1751. Heyr. 1759
Lebt inder Ehe 46J. Zeuget
13 Kinder, stirbt 1805 d.10 Jun*

*Here rests Johan George
Eisenhauer. Born at
Wilhelmsfeld in Germany
ANNO 1733, 22nd January.
Comes to NOVA SCOTIA 1751,
Marries 1759. Lives in
wedlock 46 years. Begets
13 children, dies 1805, 10th June*[2]

31

Because of the crudity of the carving and the simplicity of the images, the German stones are particularly sad. The observer can get some idea, from looking at these stones, of the total isolation of these communities from the rest of Nova Scotia. The old German stones of Lunenburg County were homemade.

Figure 32
George Jung, Lunenburg Academy,
Lunenburg Co.; slate, 1794.

Figure 33
Cathrina Maragreta Läsle,
Lunenburg Academy,
Lunenburg Co.; slate, 1808.

Figure 34
Son of Phillop Cook (?), First South,
Lunenburg Co.; slate, 1848.

32

33

34

Scottish Stones

Figure 35
John Crockett, Alma, Pictou Co.;
sandstone, 1817.

Figure 36
Alex Fraser, Alma, Pictou Co.;
sandstone, 1798.

Early Scottish stones in Nova Scotia tend to be of sandstone. They generally state from which part of Scotland (North Britain) the deceased emigrated, and also who erected (i.e., paid for) the memorial. There is rarely any decorative imagery beyond thistles, but as much written information as possible is crammed on the stone.

35

Figure 37
*Peter Fraser, old graveyard, New
Glasgow, Pictou Co.; sandstone,
1831. Knocked down and broken.*

Figure 38
*John McRae, Middle River,
Victoria Co.; sandstone, 1856.*

Figure 39
*James Adams, Truro, Colchester Co.;
sandstone; 1847.
(Photo by Barbara Robertson.)*

Figure 40
*William Lithgow, Camp Hill
Cemetery, Halifax; sandstone, 1858.
Signed: "J.H. Johnston".*

36

37

38

39

40

Trumpeting Figures

Belief in resurrection is an essential Christian doctrine. The idea is that at the end of the world there will be a general resurrection of the dead, which will be followed by an immortality either of happiness or misery. St. Paul, in a letter written to the Corinthians, added his own dramatic interpretation of the last day.

"In a moment, in a twinkling of an eye at the last trump; for the trumpet shall sound, and the dead shall be raised incorruptible, and we shall be changed" (I Cor. 15:52). Protestant theology is based firmly on the writings of Paul, and so the trumpet is a particularly Protestant symbol of resurrection. On gravestones, the image of a figure holding or blasting a trumpet shows passers-by that the deceased is there, but temporarily, and is joyfully awaiting the day of judgement.

The gravestone for the Lawson children (1772-1784) (Fig. 46) at St. Paul's Cemetery, Halifax, is of green slate (not local) and shows a symmetrical and beautifully carved pair of angels blowing horns, wearing very stylized drapery and holding something in their other hands — perhaps a pen, or wedge for clay tablets. Above them are two intertwined palm fronds and below them a four-pointed crown made of three rings. The angels perhaps represent a composite of the recording angel and the angel sounding the trumpet of resurrection. The four-pointed crown may be a symbol of mortality, an object of this world: perhaps the four points of the compass or the four ages of man. The three rings may represent the three-fold nature of man (body, soul and spirit) or birth, death and judgement. Then again, this may simply be a crown. The carver appears to have had some problem with the eyes. He seems to have been more accustomed to showing eyes face on, rather than in profile, and was not successful in making the transition. The symmetry of the carving may indicate the work of someone trained to cut heraldic devices, where crowns, drapery and intertwined fronds are common.

The Lawson children's stone was possibly carved in England, but more probably in New England. There is a stone extremely close beside it, of the same material and with the same unusual shaping on the back, which is a very dull, standard death head. I think this stone (dated 1781) for the Lawson children's grandmother was probably carved by the same hand and erected about the same time as the Lawson children's stone.

Actual physical resurrection of the body is also mentioned in both the Old and New Testaments (Job 19:26): "And though after my skin worms destroy this body, yet in my flesh shall I see God." Handley Chipman of Cornwallis, cabinetmaker by trade, who died in 1799, described in his will his hopes for a physical resurrection:

I resign . . . my Body to the Earth to be decently Buried . . . in earnest hope and humble Confidence of a Glorious Resurrection. Trusting and believing that whenever this my Clayey [sic] Tabernacle which must shortly very shortly be desolved into dust shall be raised again by the mighty power of God a shining and spiritual Body where the human nature shall appear in its fullest lustre and dignity and the image of God in man shall receive its last and finishing stroke of beauty and perfection this corruptible shall put on incoruption and this mortal shall put on immortality and both Soul and Body being again United, shall be admitted into the immediate presence of God, where is fullness of joy and where are Rivers of pleasure for evermore Amen. [1]

On the gravestone of Elizabeth Riggs in Liverpool (sandstone, 1815) we find a very skilfully carved representation of a female form rising through clouds and reaching out toward distant rays of the new dawn (Fig. 47). Mrs. Riggs was the daughter of John Payzant, a New-Light minister, and the niece of Henry Alline, the New-Light revival leader of Nova Scotia during the American Revolution. Thus it is no accident that her gravestone depicts her body, not just her soul, rising on the last day. This is, however, an unusual gravestone image.

Figure 41
Mary/Freke Bulkeley, St. Paul's
Cemetery, Halifax; slate, 1796.
Foot panel (see Figure 102).
(Photo by R. Merrick.)

Figure 42
John McPhee, Nine Mile River,
Hants Co.; sandstone, 1811.

41

42

Figure 43
Nancy Dalloway, West Amherst,
Cumberland Co.; sandstone, 1793.
Broken.

Figure 44
"The trumpet shall sound and the
dead shall be raised".
Middle Sackville, New Brunswick;
sandstone, 1794.

Figure 45
Michael Spur, Annapolis Royal,
Annapolis Co.; sandstone, 1804.

43

44

45

46

e Jies Interr'd the Bodjes of the Childr

47

The Neo-Classical Revival

Following the upheaval of the American Revolution, there was in the United States a feeling of beginning again, and in the new republic trend-setters looked to other republics for a model. The republics of the ancient world seemed to suit the purpose. At about the same time European interest in the visual aspects of the classical period was revived with the first archaeological discoveries at Pompeii and Herculaneum — about 1750. This "neo-classical" revival (c. 1780-1830) affected fashion in all branches of visual arts, from architecture to clothing, even exerting an influence on gravestone art.

The most obvious example is the introduction of the secular symbol of the urn. The funerary urn as an object was not familiar to most inhabitants of late eighteenth century Nova Scotia. The Greeks had used such sophisticated receptacles for human remains, but it was an ancient custom. It would appear that local gravestone carvers jumped on the urn as a death symbol because it was relatively easy to carve. For instance, D. Shaw, working in the vicinity of Amherst, cut in sandstone a very simple outline of an urn, enclosing the initials of the deceased (Fig. 48).

The earliest images of urns on gravestones appear on imported stones; for example the Snow Parker stone in Liverpool (1794), probably carved by Maxcy in Salem, Massachusetts (Fig. 49). By about 1800 the urn was well established as a symbol for the earthly repository of the body.

48

Figure 48
William Pipes, West Amherst,
Cumberland Co.; sandstone, 1804
Signed: "D. Shaw fecit".

Figure 49
Snow Parker, Liverpool, Queens Co.;
slate, 1794.

Figure 50
John Clements, Chebogue,
Yarmouth Co.; slate, 1805.

Figure 51
Reuben George Clements, Chebogue,
Yarmouth Co.; slate, 1822.

49

50

51

Willow and Urn

Figure 52
William Cogswell Jr., Upper
Canard, Kings Co.; sandstone,
1824.

52

The willow tree has long been a symbol of mourning. The psalmist tells us that the Jews in captivity "hanged their harps upon the willows" in sign of mourning (Psalm 137). The very term "weeping" willow is enough to account for its emblematic character. In the Victorian language of flowers the willow meant the forsaken.[1] And so in gravestone art the image of the willow (the bereaved) began to appear leaning mournfully over the urn.

Beyond the symbol of bereavement is the implication of healing. In Christian symbolism the willow continues to flourish no matter how many of its branches are cut. Thus it also becomes a symbol of the gospel of Christ.[2] Boiled willow leaves are supposed to produce a healing effect similar to aspirin.

The image of the willow and urn does not seem to have reached the popularity peak in Nova Scotia that it did in Massachusetts.[3] Willows and urns are found in sandstone and white stone from the 1830's, 40's and later. A number of willows and urns on slate from the early part of the nineteenth century are found in the vicinity of Yarmouth, but these are obviously imported from New England.

Why this image did not catch on in Nova Scotia may be explained by the fact that it first appeared in New England in the period immediately following the American Revolution and was very common by the time of the War of 1812 — an overall period of political strain between Halifax and Boston which must have discouraged the transferal of design ideas. This period marks the end of cultural dependence on New England.[4] Willow and urn images in Nova Scotia are generally much later and produced by commercial monument works.

Figure 53
Sarah DeWolf, Hebron,
Yarmouth Co.; white stone, 1852.

Figure 54
Elizabeth Poole, Old Church of
England graveyard, Yarmouth; slate,
1839. Attributed to J.T. Archer.

Figure 55
Hannah Boutilier, Hacketts Cove,
Halifax Co.; white stone, 1849.

Figure 56
Arabella Savage, Cheboque,
Yarmouth Co.; slate, 1848
Attributed to J. T. Archer.

53

55
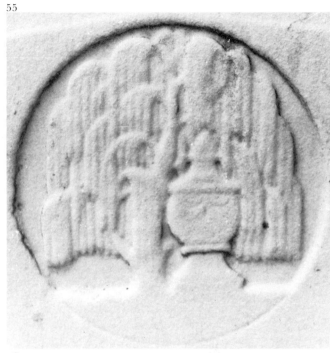

54

56

The Rural Cemetery Movement

Early Christian burial grounds had been called cemeteries, from the Greek word meaning sleeping place. These were outside city walls and unconnected with churches. Gradually burial areas began to have religious connections and churchyards were increasingly used for this purpose. By the late 18th century churchyards and vaults had become overcrowded — so full that they were unhealthy and quite disgusting places to visit. Yet, what came to be known as the rural cemetery movement began, not in London or any of the old and crowded cities of Europe, but in Boston.

Although the connection between contagious disease and infested old burial grounds was a known fact in the early 1800's, no one bothered to do anything about it until Dr. Jacob Bigelow of Boston, tired of trying to convince the city to act, began on his own to interest people in the concept of a cemetery. His idea was to purchase a large area of land and have it maintained as a park, supervised by salaried staff, and open to anyone who wished to purchase a lot. Working with the Massachusetts Horticultural Society, Bigelow pushed the idea. However, it was the concept of this new cemetery as an instructional centre that had great popular appeal, not any argument concerning health improvements. What better opportunity for moral learning than the contemplation of the dead, not in horror, but in a natural situation where the beauties of nature are combined with art. The rural cemetery movement was part of a much larger period of change in public views of nature, which saw also the beginning of municipal parks.[1]

Mount Auburn Cemetery, in Cambridge, Mass., was opened in 1831. Although not in fact the first rural cemetery, it was the first to get widespread publicity. Postcards exist of Mount Auburn. It was the place to go for an afternoon drive and to admire the gardens. Many effusive personal descriptions of the beauty of Mount Auburn were printed. With this kind of advertising, it is not surprising that cemeteries based on the idea of Mount Auburn quickly appeared all over North America.[2]

In Nova Scotia there are hundreds of rural cemeteries, the oldest probably being Camp Hill Cemetery in Halifax. Of course, what was rural in 1844 when Camp Hill was opened, is quite urban now, but the term "rural cemetery" still applies. St. Paul's burial ground in Halifax, which was closed in the same year, had become overcrowded, slimy and neglected.[3]

In the original charter of Mount Auburn, slate was forbidden as a gravemarking material. The reason is uncertain, perhaps because of its connection with the gruesome death heads of the seventeenth century. For whatever reason, this idea carried over to all those new cemeteries which had taken Mount Auburn for a model. In replacing slate, "white stone" became the vogue.

Figure 57
Detail of a plan of Mountain
Cemetery, Yarmouth, 1861.
(Collection of the Yarmouth County
Historical Society)

57

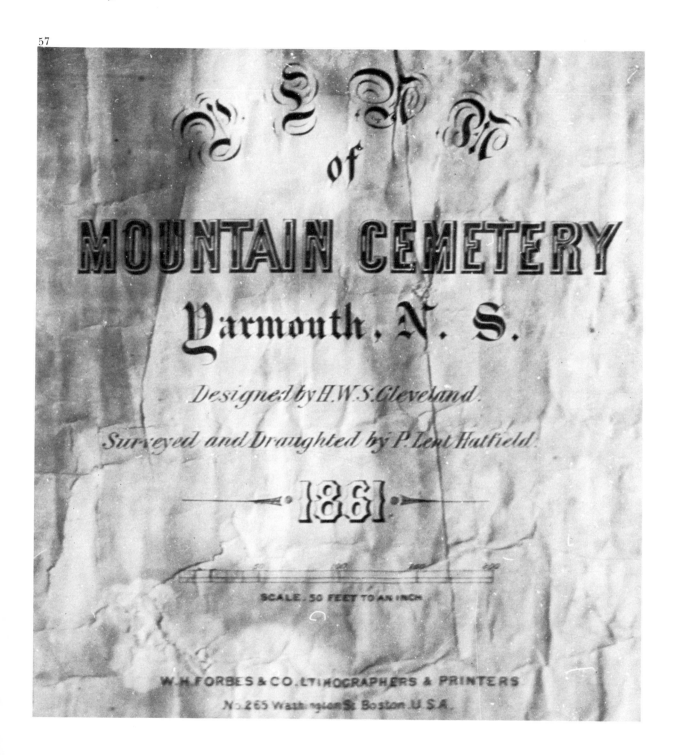

White Stone

White stone has always had a special appeal. People idling along a beach will handle or pocket the white stones, often without knowing why. The association between white stone and commemoration of the dead is a long one. Covering graves with white stone was a Bronze Age sepulchral practise.[1] In Biblical times white stone had come to mean a reward, or in judgement, a pardon. "To him that overcometh will I give to eat of the hidden manna, and will give him a white stone, and in the stone a new name written . . ." (Rev. 2:17).

The change in public attitudes to burial that led to establishing rural cemeteries also affected gravestone fashion. In these cemeteries there was space to erect large monuments. As the marble statues of antiquity survived, so would the memorials of middle class Victorians survive. At least that was the idea. White marble became the standard stone in Victorian cemeteries.

Marble may have been used because of its cost — an external and lasting demonstration of the wealth of the deceased. It may have been used because it was visually attractive, it could be quarried in North America, and it was the traditional material for sculpture. The "no slate" clause in the charter of Mount Auburn certainly helped to promote marble. As well, the symbolic significance of white stone added to the popular appeal of marble as a memorial, whether or not people were aware of it. The Biblical attribution of white stone to a pardon or reward, when applied to a white memorial, implies that the dead one is pardoned for his earthly sins and finds a reward in death — perhaps heavenly bliss.

Whatever the reason, white marble took over cemeteries. In Nova Scotia it was used from about 1845 to about 1920.

The variety found in Nova Scotian cemeteries is not the kind of marble found in Italy, or even Vermont. Marble is a name loosely applied to limestone which varies from mostly calcite at one end of the scale, to mostly dolomite at the other. The calcite variety is what we know as Italian marble.[2] Dolomite contains magnesium which makes it more susceptible to erosion. In time, dolomite begins to crumble and behave like sandstone when left to weather, while calcite does not change. Thus many of our dolomitic gravestones have become illegible and the finer details of the carving imperceptible.

From about 1840 we find more and more commercial monument works in Nova Scotia. These were still small shops where carvers worked with hammer and chisel, mainly on white stone — for example, Thomas Wesley, whose Halifax Marble Works was producing "Monuments, Tomb Tables, Gravestones and Baptismal Fonts" by 1863.

With these commercial marble works, gravestone images became more and more "off the rack" and showed less and less of the individual carver's skill. Standard images such as a sheaf of wheat for old age, an open book, a broken bud or a lamb (for a child), dominated the industry. The symbol of hands (to take one specific image) in different poses, show individual carver's input.

Figure 58
Worn stone, St. Paul's Cemetery,
Halifax; white stone, n.d.

Figure 59
Advertisement for Halifax Marble
Works (Thomas Wesley) in
Hutchinson's Halifax Directory,
1863. (Photo by R. Merrick)

58

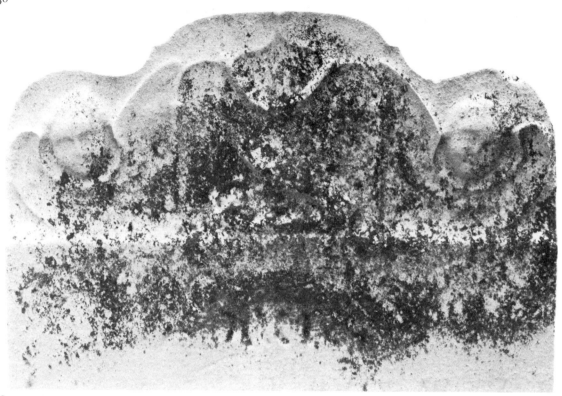

59

Hands

Hands in white stone are extremely common. Frequently they show one finger pointing to the sky, implying the general direction the soul has taken. These are often accompanied by some explanatory text, such as "Gone Home".

Handshakes usually represent the last farewell on earth, or perhaps the hand of God reaching down to claim his own.

The interesting thing about hands on gravestones is the way in which the carver chooses to vary small details — cuff and sleeve patterns and textures, for example. Note the same basic hand in Figures 60 to 66.

Because hands are so common, there are several curiosities to be found. The stones for William and Elizabeth Haskell, Chegoggin, Yarmouth Co., c. 1874, (Fig. 67) show a hand on each reaching out, and should probably have been set so as to be reaching toward each other, suggesting they were "united above", as it were. This did not happen, and they appear to be turning away from one another. On the John Smith stone, Truro, c. 1857, (Fig. 68) the carver, H. E. Smith of Pictou, seems to have gotten his stencil or prototype turned around: the handshake is upside down.

Hands in sandstone are contemporary with white stone. In Pictou County in particular, where sandstone was perhaps more accessible and so used more than white stone, you find some very peculiar, even crude, hands. See for instance the Mary Fraser stone, East River St. Mary's, Pictou County, 1866 (Fig. 69) which is sandstone, probably carved in New Glasgow.

On older stones, hands are not the predominant image, but are used to emphasize part of the script. A tiny hand on the Hannah Harris stone, Clementsport, Digby Co. (slate, 1826) points to the year (Fig. 70). There are several examples where one stone is used to mark two graves and information about the second death, usually that of the wife, appears as an afterthought, added to her husband's monument with a casual hand pointing to her resting place. The William/Jemima Alline stone, Wolfville, Kings County (sandstone, c. 1820) shows one such hand (Fig. 71).

Figure 60
Mary Dodd, Nine Mile River, Hants Co.; white stone, 1874.

Figure 61
Hand and Book, Broad Cove, Inverness Co. No name or date noted; probably cut by Coll Campbell, c. 1900.

Figure 62
Sarah Ann Trefry, Chebogue, Yarmouth Co; white stone, 1858.

Figure 63
John Moore, Hacketts Cove, Halifax Co.; white stone, 1887.

60

62

63

61

Figure 64
Catherine Miller, Hacketts Cove,
Halifax Co.; white stone, 1887.

Figure 65
John Caldwell, Nine Mile River,
Hants Co.; white stone, 1874.

Figure 66
Elias Oxner, Lunenburg Academy,
Lunenburg Co., white stone, 1859.

Figure 67
William/Elizabeth Haskell,
Chegoggin, Yarmouth Co.;
white stone, c. 1874.

64

66

65

67

Figure 68
*John Smith, Truro, Colchester Co.;
white stone, c. 1857.
(Photo by Barbara Robertson)*

Figure 69
*Mary Fraser, East River St. Mary's,
Pictou Co.; sandstone, 1866.*

69

68

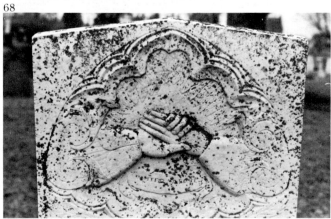

Figure 70
Hannah Harris, Clementsport,
Annapolis Co.; slate, 1826.

Figure 71
William/Jemima Alline, Wolfville,
Kings Co.; sandstone, 1820.

70

71

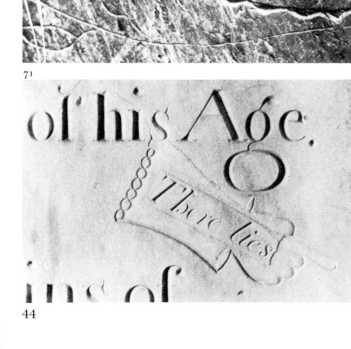

44

Flowers

Flowers were also popular images in white stone.
There was a peculiar Victorian idea of giving each
variety of plant a symbolic meaning. Luckily for us
these interpretations were written up in dictionary
form but almost everyone at the time knew that a
crocus meant cheerfulness, or a white violet, delicacy,[1]
and so composed bouquets with care. Often flowers
depicted on gravestones are stylistic blooms, perhaps
in the form of a permanent wreath. Many are
recognizable varieties.

Beyond the Victorian language of flowers there is the
more obvious symbolic use of flowers — the broken
bud, for example, usually commemorating a child cut
down before its life had bloomed (Fig. 73). Verses on
the stone tend to support this kind of interpretation.

Flowers are also symbols of resurrection in their own
right. Evidence of God's power is in the works of
returning nature, flowers and fruits in their season.
This is an example to us of how easily He can make
those that are in the dust awake to life.

Figure 72
Darling Eva Doull, Camp Hill
Cemetery, Halifax; white stone,
1872.

Figure 73
Jonas Johnson, Camp Hill Cemetery,
Halifax; white stone, 1867.

72

73
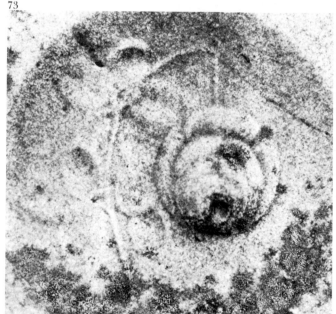

Masonic Imagery

Memorials for men who were members of the secret fraternal order of Free and Accepted Masons often depict masonic symbols. The earlier stones are more elaborate, showing the sun, moon, stars, a huge eyeball, an open book, a ladder, compass and square, string of initials, etc. These mean something to Masons.[1] The most Masonic stone I've seen is the Abner Stowell stone (sandstone, 1821) in St. Paul's Cemetery, Halifax, carved by David Kinnear (Fig. 74). It is obvious from this stone that Kinnear's background was in architectural stonecarving.

75

Figure 74
Abner Stowell, St. Paul's Cemetery,
Halifax; sandstone, 1821.
Signed: "D. Kinnear".

Figure 75
William Forrester, Clyde River,
Shelburne Co.; sandstone, 1825.

Figure 76
William McKinnon, St. George's
Church, Sydney, C.B.; slate, 1811.

Figure 77
William A. Metzner, Lunenburg
Cemetery, Lunenburg Co.;
white stone, 1864.

Cast Iron

Cast iron grave markers are found in Nova Scotia dating from about 1845. Despite the fact that cast iron was durable, adaptable and relatively cheap, not to mention easier to ship than stone, it did not catch on as a popular memorial material. Perhaps people were distrustful of a new material used for an ancient custom. Although cast iron markers could be mass produced, once a pattern existed, by simply changing the name and date lines, there are proportionately few to be found in Nova Scotia. Those that do exist were cast, for the most part, in the foundries of William Johns and W. D. Faulkner.[1]

The William Johns Foundry of Halifax was one of the earliest making decorative castings in Nova Scotia.[2] Although in operation by 1835, Johns was most active in the 1840's and 50's. The simplest of his cast iron markers are plain information panels, with raised letters and decorated with a swirl, bordered by two thinner, almost architectural panels. The whole, surmounted by three points, stands upright in the ground by means of two legs extending from the bottom corners.

There are about a dozen such cast iron markers in Camp Hill Cemetery, several of which have unfortunately rusted and the raised lettering has worn beyond legibility (Fig. 78).

There are other William Johns markers around the province — see, for example, the Louisa Card memorial, (Windsor, 1845) which has been knocked down (Fig. 79).

Johns also produced fancy work in his grave marker line. The Luke Hamilton memorial at Centre Gore, Hants Co. (cast iron, 1852) (Fig. 80) is an interesting example.

Cast iron grave markers marked W. H. Faulkner (registered 1884) are spread all over the province. These consist of lattice work, some of which are topped by a complete three dimensional hand pointing to the heavens (Fig. 81). Data concerning the deceased was probably on paper fixed to a small panel under glass. In every case the paper has washed away to nothing. The great advantage of Faulkner markers was that they could be sold anywhere — through an undertaker or even a general store, and the paper filled in and added as appropriate.

Figure 78
Cast iron grave markers, Camp Hill
Cemetery, Halifax, late 1840's.

Figure 79
Louisa Card, Windsor, Hants Co.;
cast iron, 1845.

Figure 80
Luke Hamilton, Centre Gore,
Hants Co.; cast iron, 1852.

78

79

80

Figure 81
Two cast iron grave markers, cast by
W. H. Faulkner after 1884.
(a) Scotsburn, Pictou Co.
(b) Parrsboro, Cumberland Co.

81a

81b

White Bronze

White bronze markers are more common than cast iron. These are also of cast metal — probably mainly zinc — and received wide distribution throughout Nova Scotia in the late 1880's and early 1890's.

The advantages of white bronze are best explained by the following piece of promotional advertising:[1]

White Bronze Solves one of the great questions of the day, being pronounced by scientists as practically indestructable. It does not corrode or change its color; moss will not grow on it, and as it does not absorb moisture, it is not affected by frost.

Time has proven these statements true.

White bronze markers are usually bluish, very elaborate, and cast to imitate stone (unlike most cast iron markers). Occasionally they are marked "White Bronze Co. St. Thomas, Ont". These differ visually from stone in that they don't erode, and are hollow. Such markers were probably ordered from Ontario through a local distributor and cast there, inexpensively, with removable name and date panels.

White bronze markers are commonly obelisk-shaped although there exists a cheaper version — a small upright panel, generally for a child, with the usual raised cast decoration and sometimes an almost scratched-on motif on the reverse.

Figure 82
(a) White bronze grave marker, Grand Pré, Kings Co.
(b) Cast mark.

82a

82b

Figure 83
Nathaniel Hogg, Chebogue,
Yarmouth Co.; white bronze, 1887.

Figure 84
Arthur Hood, Church of England
graveyard, Shelburne; white bronze,
1887. Reverse.
(Photo by Mary Harvey)

83

84

Granite

In the last decades of the nineteenth century polished granite began to be popular as a gravestone material. This was only possible through the development of pneumatic tools, as granite is an extremely hard stone. Raw granite is imported to Nova Scotia from India, Sweden, Finland, North Africa, the United States and centres in Canada. It arrives in large blocks weighing up to as much as eight tons. There are also granite quarries in Nictaux, Annapolis County, and Shelburne.[1] The largest importers and distributors of granite in Nova Scotia at the present time are Tingley Monuments Ltd. of Amherst, Heritage Memorials of Windsor and W. T. Dauphinee Ltd. of Shelburne. Decorative details are applied by sandblasting through rubber stencils.

85

86

Curiosities

Garden of Eden Lady — In the Garden of Eden Cemetery at Moose River, Pictou County, stands a very curious statue. This commemorates a woman of the Sutherland family and was carved by James King of New Glasgow and Halifax[1] (Fig. 87). King carved this monument from a photograph, and family tradition has it that he was never paid for the job. The base came from the W. R. MacKenzie Monument Works, New Glasgow.

The Garden of Eden Lady, probably carved in 1893, is very stiff and disproportionate, with enormous hands. She has become something of a local landmark.

Mrs. Webster — The Margaret McNaught Webster monument (Fig. 88) in Town Point Cemetery, Chebogue, Yarmouth County, is curious because separate from the gravestone is a life-size marble statue. This depicts the prone Margaret McNaught supposedly as Frederick A. Webster first saw her in a Scottish field, dozing on a sheaf of wheat, sickle in hand.[2] They were married in Halifax in the spring of 1834.[3] The statute (particularly the feet) has been chipped away by perverse souvenir hunters. The separate monument which gives Mrs. Webster's vital statistics is a granite obelisk with purple slate panels.

The Captain John Phillips stone at Margaree Centre, Inverness County, (granite, 1854) (Fig. 89), is an amputated millstone. The inscription is very shallow because of the hardness of the stone. The grindstone has no apparent connection with his life, however, as he was a captain of a schooner trading between Newfoundland and Cape Breton.[4]

At Stewiacke, Hants County, stands a very impressive stone to the memory of Thomas Bell who died in 1867 (Fig. 90). This is a normal white stone monument, but it is cased in granite, cut to resemble a tree, or tree roots, with all the branches lopped off. There is another such stone for Capt. Stephen Stoddard (1864) not quite as well made, at Mount Denson, Hants County. Both came from the shop of James Wood, Jr., of Windsor.

There are a number of gravestones at Petite Riviere in Lunenburg County which are shaped and smoothed but show no incised or raised marks. This I thought very curious until I found one that still had traces of black paint on it (Fig. 91). The name and date are not decipherable.

Figure 87
(a,b,c) Mary Sutherland Morrison,
Moose River, Pictou Co.; sandstone,
1882/1893. (a) J. King's own
photograph, courtesy Mrs. S. Miller.

87a

87b

87c

Figure 89
Captain John Phillips, Margaree
Centre, Inverness Co.; granite,
1854.

Figure 90
Thomas Bell, Stewiacke, Hants Co.;
white stone and granite, 1864.

Figure 91
Painted stone, Petite Riviere,
Lunenburg Co.; illegible.

89

91

90

The Hay Family of Halifax

Among the blackened eighteenth century stones of St. Paul's Cemetery, Halifax, are some of the earliest native carved gravestones. One of the first stone artists was James Hay, "Stone Cutter and Carver lately from Scotland" who carved the Robert Campbell stone, (Fig. 93) probably in the summer of 1776.[1] This is made of local slate or "ironstone" which is usually very dark and mottled with rusty spots running through it. The Robert Campbell stone shows a raised winged head of an adult with fine, curly eighteenth century hair, poppy eyes, two rosettes or flowers stemming from below the wings, and a very detailed flower border (Fig. 93a). The James Clark, (Fig. 94) (slate, 1777), Patrick Britt (Fig. 95) (slate 1757?), and Elizabeth Peise (slate, 1777) stones, all at St. Paul's, are similar to the Robert Campbell stone but the lettering is awkward and the decorative carving details not as fine. These may be the work of an apprentice in the Hay shop.

By 1780 James Hay was renting in a building adjoining the Ordnance Store.[2] He seems to have been still in business in 1792 and 1793 when he was listed in the Assessment Rolls of Halifax.[3] Although I can find no later reference to James Hay, in those Assessment Rolls there appears another Hay — John Hay, mason.[4]

John Hay was the son of James Hay.[5] He was admitted as an ordinary member to the North British Society in 1799.[6] In 1803 John Hay was paid for making a gravestone for Edmond Phelan of Halifax.[7] He obtained a commission as a lieutenant in the militia in 1807;[8] he owned property on Sackville St. in 1817 valued at £200; and more on Upper Water St. by 1819.[9] However, in May of 1820, one John Hay of Halifax, mason, "a native of Scotland and a widower" applied for a Crown Land grant of five hundred acres. His request was denied with the explanation that ". . . his trade as a mason will afford him a more certain support than the cultivation of the forest lands which I fear he is not acquainted with".[10] This is the last I can find of John Hay. Nor have I found any specific examples of his work.

93a

93b

Figure 92
Advertisement for James Hay in the
Nova Scotia Gazette and Weekly
Chronicle September 17, 1776.
(Collection of the Massachusetts
Historical Society)

Figure 93
Robert Campbell, St. Paul's
Cemetery, Halifax; slate, 1775. (a)
(Photo by William Inglis Morse) (b)
Side border detail.
(Photo by R. Merrick)

92

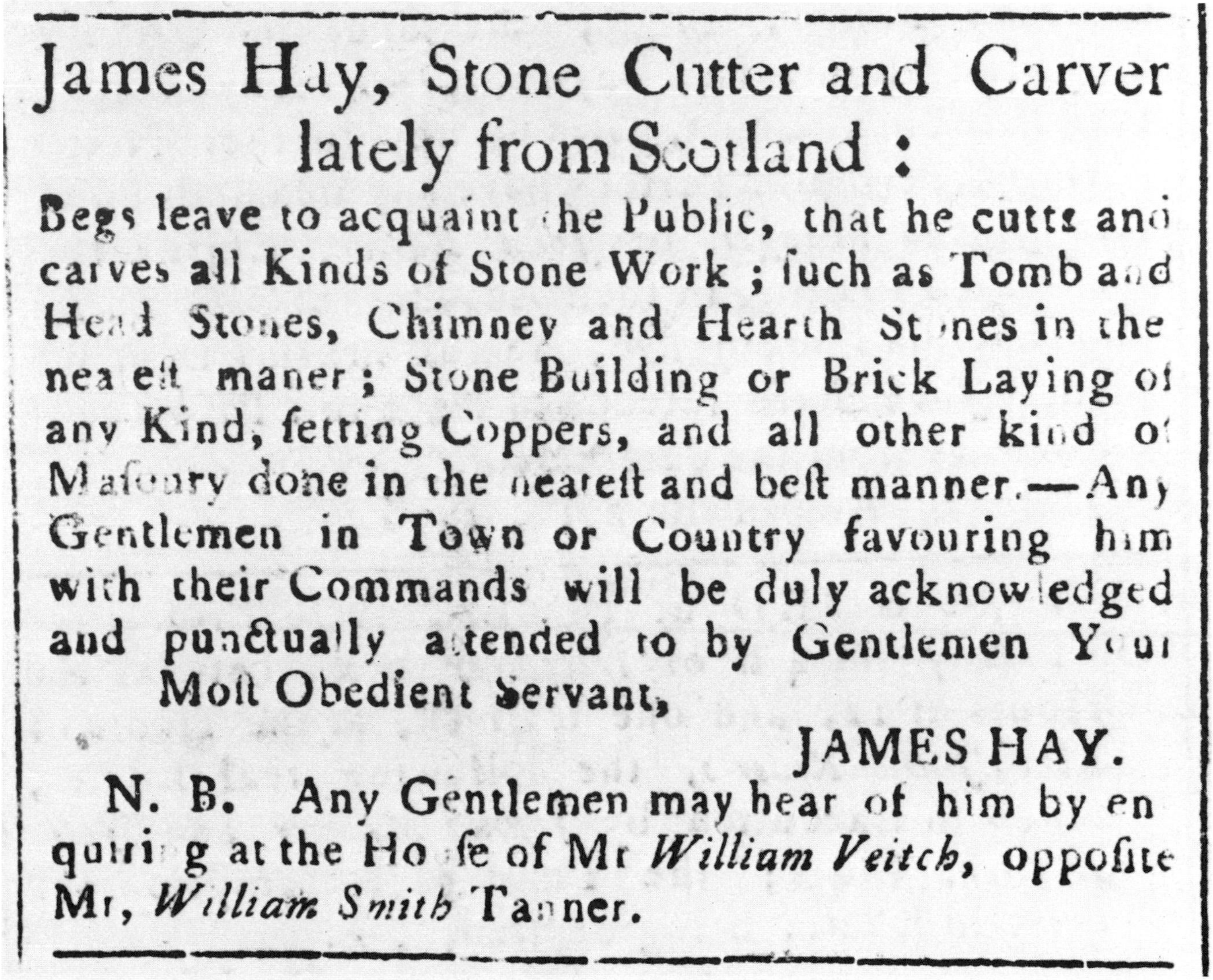

James Hay, Stone Cutter and Carver lately from Scotland :

Begs leave to acquaint the Public, that he cutts and carves all Kinds of Stone Work ; such as Tomb and Head Stones, Chimney and Hearth Stones in the neatest maner ; Stone Building or Brick Laying of any Kind, setting Coppers, and all other kind of Masonry done in the neatest and best manner.—Any Gentlemen in Town or Country favouring him with their Commands will be duly acknowledged and punctually attended to by Gentlemen Your Most Obedient Servant,

JAMES HAY.

N. B.   Any Gentlemen may hear of him by enquiring at the House of Mr *William Veitch*, opposite Mr, *William Smith* Tanner.

Figure 94
James Clark, St. Paul's Cemetery,
Halifax; slate, 1777.

HERE LIETH THE BODY OF
JAMES CLARK WHO DEPARTED
THIS LIFE FEBRUARY 2, 1777 AGD
46 YEARS
The Seas shall waste the Skies in smoke decay
Rocks fall to Dust and Mountains melt away
But fixd His Word, His saving Power Remains
Thy Realm forever lasts thy own Messiah Reigns
POPE

There are in St. Paul's Cemetery, Halifax, a number of stones from the late 1700's very similar to the Robert Campbell stone, but even more of them resemble the John Clewley stone, also carved by James Hay[11] (Fig. 96, 97). The Clewley stone is sandstone and the cherub head is totally separate from the wings. Note the M-shape of the wings, which are in three layers. Note also the elaborate border around the inscription. Other stones with a very similar head and wings, but lacking any other imagery beyond stylized rosettes at the top corners, stand at St. Paul's and by the Little Dutch Church on Brunswick St. These tend to be later in period and presumably had cost less. Beyond Halifax, the Margaret Copeland stone (slate, 1793) (Fig. 99) in New Glasgow is a good example of a later stone; although there are several in Lunenburg, Windsor and other scattered locations. Another distinctive detail on stones from the Hay workshop is the letter "H" in "Here lies". The H's all have a squiggle in the cross bar (Fig. 100). The top panel of the Adam and Eve stone has such an H.

The Adam and Eve tombstone at St. Paul's is possibly a product of the Hay workshop. This commemorates Mary Bulkeley, wife of Provincial Secretary Richard Bulkeley, who died in 1775. Her obituary mentions only that "her remains were decently interr'd."[12] Richard himself merited a prestigious intramural burial site at St. Paul's Church, complete with marble wall plaque. The date of the Adam and Eve is confused by the addition of Bulkeley's son, Freke, who died in 1796, and the memorial was probably erected after that time. On the top piece is an heraldic emblem, the bull's head coat of arms of the Bulkeley family (as loosely interpreted in North America[13]). The heraldic imagery is not as well carved as that on the Winckworth Tonge stone (sandstone, 1792) right beside it. This makes me think the Bulkeley stone could possibly be the work of two individuals — or perhaps made by the carver of the stones of James Clark, Patrick Britt, and others. The borders on the top piece resemble closely the borders on the Robert Campbell stone; however, the Bulkeley is very worn from nearly two hundred years of snow and rain falling on the carved slate surface.

Most interesting, however, are the two end panels of the Bulkeley stone. The foot panel depicts a complete prostrate skeleton surmounted by a full, but seated, figure rising to the call of another figure standing to the left, presumably the angel Gabriel, blowing an enormous trumpet. The Biblical text for this could very well be I Corinthians 15:22: "For as in Adam all die, even so in Christ shall all be made alive". The head panel shows Adam and Eve (wearing what resembles swimming trunks) standing on either side of a richly loaded apple tree. A serpent is wound around the tree trunk and leers from among the branches, an apple in its mouth. Two little bushes, possibly representing the Garden, stand in the bottom corners and a round rayed sun looks down from the top left corner. All the figures are in quite high relief. The end panels have, in addition, a wide and elaborate border. The whole was probably taken from a printed illustration; for example *The Child's Guide* printed in London in 1725 shows a very similar Adam and Eve.[14]

The image of Adam and Eve in gravestone art is not unique to the Bulkeley stone. A similar example is the Sarah Swan stone, (slate, 1767), Bristol Rhode Island, (Fig. 104). (The figures of Adam and Eve on the Sarah Swan stone are wearing trunks made of leaves.) In the parking area by St. Mary's Church, across Spring Garden Road from St. Paul's Cemetery, there is another slate Adam and Eve gravestone panel[15] (Fig. 102). This is set into the asphalt and was probably left there when the Catholic graveyard was destroyed to build the school. This Adam and Eve seems to have been made in the same workshop as the Bulkeley stone; however, there are slight variations. The wide border is undecorated and the positioning of the

61

Figure 95
*Patrick Britt, St. Paul's Cemetery,
Halifax; slate, 1757.*

Figure 96
*John Clewley, St. Paul's Cemetery,
Halifax; sandstone, 1783.*

Figure 97
*James Hay's account against the
estate of John Clewley, March, 1783.*

Figure 98
*Peter Artz, Little Dutch Church,
Halifax; slate, 1792.*

95

97

98

96

Figure 99
Margaret Copland, old graveyard,
New Glasgow, Pictou Co.; slate,
1793.

Figure 100
Jean Cater, St. Paul's Cemetery,
Halifax; sandstone, n.d.

Figure 101
"In Adam's fall/We sinned all",
The Child's Guide, 1725.

100

99

101

Figure 102
Mary/Freke Bulkeley, St. Paul's
Cemetery, Halifax; slate, 1796.
(a) Head panel (b) Foot panel (c) Top
(d) Top border detail.

102a

102b

102c

102d

Figure 103
End panel of a tombstone, depicting
Adam and Eve, Catholic burying
ground, Spring Garden Road,
Halifax; slate. No name, no date,
c. 1795.
(Now in the collection of the Nova
Scotia Museum.)

Figure 104
Sarah Swann, Bristol, Rhode Island;
slate, 1767.
(Photo courtesy of Dr. A. I. Ludwig)

Figure 107
Map showing distribution of Peter
Hay stones.

figures and the hair is quite different. Unfortunately, generations of school children stomping on it have obliterated many of the finer details. If these two Adam and Eves were not carved by James Hay, their carver was greatly influenced by him.

The Susanna McDonald stone in Windsor (sandstone, 1777) (Fig. 105) was very probably carved by James Hay. The front is plain (the "H" also) but the back is extremely ornate, showing a coat of arms bordered by very deep three-part swirls, derived from heraldic manteling, and the same old crossed bones and hourglass. Most interesting are the flowers at the shoulders. Compare these to the flowers under the wings at the top of the Robert Campbell stone (Fig. 93a). The great similarities cannot be ignored, especially when you consider the difference in material.

The Richard McHeffey stone, also in Windsor (sandstone, 1790) (Fig. 106) is more stilted in comparison. The ribbon doesn't flow, the fringe is stiff, the roping on the edge is flat. It appears to come from the same shop as the Susanna McDonald stone, but either carved by someone else (John?) or as a cheaper version.

Peter Hay (1750-1842) — Peter Hay's relationship to James and John is not certain — possibly he was another son of James. He had land on Upper Water and Argyle Streets in Halifax in 1817, Upper Water and Gerrish Streets in 1818, in a place identified as "suburbs" by 1821, and a workshop on Jacob Street in 1822.[16] There are gravestones signed by Peter Hay in Shelburne (1812), near Ottawa House outside Parrsboro (1822), Wolfville (1825) and in Lunenburg and Parrsboro (1836).[17] This is an impressive geographic distribution of products for the period, if you consider transportation routes.

All of these are large pieces of sandstone with standard imagery of the time — urns and drapery in high relief. The nicest is the Alex Cocken stone in Shelburne with its fancy lettering in a slightly raised oval surmounted by palm branches and an urn (Fig. 110).

107

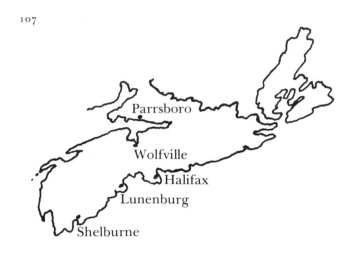

James William Hay This James Hay, who died in 1843 and was a son of Peter Hay,[18] also made gravestones. There is one signed by him (1836) in Liverpool which shows nothing distinctive, nor any decorative details. Another sandstone memorial signed by James Hay is in Windsor, dated 1835 (Fig. 111). This shows a standard raised urn but it is otherwise quite plain.

105

106

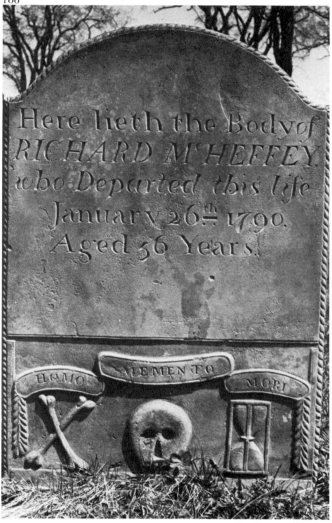

108

The Subscriber

HAVING commenced Business in the
Stone and Brick Laying, and Stone
Cutting Line, begs leave to solicit a share
of public patronage; and assures those who
may be pleased to employ him, that he will
use his best endeavours to give satisfaction,
and that their commands shall be attended to
with punctuality and dispatch.

N. B. Tomb Stones cut and letterd in
the neatest manner.

PETER HAY.

Halifax, March 11.

Figure 109
Catherine Ratchford, Wolfville,
Kings Co.; sandstone, 1825.

Figure 110
Alex Cocken, Church of England
graveyard, Shelburne, sandstone,
1812. Signed: "P. Hay".
(Photo by Barbara Robertson)

Figure 111
Elizabeth Scott, Windsor, Hants Co.;
sandstone, 1835.
Signed: "James Hay/Halifax, N.S."

109

111

110

The Seaman Family of Horton and Cumberland

112

113

Abraham Seaman (1767-1848) was a son of Jacamiah Seaman, a Loyalist from New York who settled in Cumberland County.[1] Abraham came to Horton, where he married Mercy, a daughter of Timothy Bishop, probably about 1794. He later returned to Pugwash, Cumberland County, but his sons Thomas Lewis, Jacomiah, and Abraham settled in Horton.[2] The first Abraham Seaman seems to have been making gravestones in Horton/Cornwallis district from about 1812 to 1821.[3] The Ezekiel Woodworth (Fig. 112) (1812), and Timothy Barnaby (1821) stones, both at Chipman's Corner, Kings County, and the Cyrus Peck (1812) stone at Kentville are known to have been carved by Abraham Seaman.[4] They have a great deal in common with many, many stones in that area and from that period, as well as with a few around Amherst. The finely incised angel heads have strange distinctive eye detail which makes them appear to be wearing glasses.[5] The wings, forehead and nose are all on one plane, but the cheeks are cut in further for some slight shaping. The outline of the wings very neatly turns into a collar under the chin. Seaman could have been taking his prototype from the Annapolis carver — they make an interesting comparison.

The John Bishop stone (sandstone, 1815) (Fig. 113) on Maple Street by the Gaspereau River in Kings County was also cut by Abraham Seaman.[6] This piece of sandstone has cracked, water has gotten into it and the top surface is flaking off, but the carving details are still visible. Note the characteristic "cherub with glasses" and also the way the neck and body turn cleverly into an hourglass — universal symbol of the passing of time, and thus of mortality.
Stones for children, depicting a small bird perched on crossed branches, were also carved by Abraham Seaman. Again there are several of these in the Windsor to Kentville area. See, for example, the Winckworth Tonge stone (sandstone, 1795) (Fig. 114) in Windsor; and especially the Edward N. Seaman stone (sandstone, 1815) (Fig. 115) in Wolfville, for the son of Abraham and Mercy Seaman. The crossed branches, reminiscent of crossed bones, could also

Figure 114
Winckworth Tonge, Windsor,
Hants Co.; sandstone, 1795.

Figure 115
Edward N. Seaman, Wolfville,
Kings Co.; sandstone, 1815.

Figure 116
John Bishop, Wolfville, Kings Co.;
sandstone; 1785.

Figure 117
Isaac Deschamps, Windsor,
Hants Co.; sandstone, 1805.

114

115

116

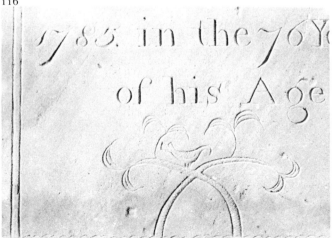

117

Figure 118
Dr. Jacob Walton, Upper Canard,
Kings Co.; sandstone, 1840.

Figure 119
Charles W. Harrison, Grand Pré,
Kings Co.; white stone, 1867.
Signed: "T.L.S./Horton".

118

119

represent the bereaved parents. This interpretation is possibly reading too much into the symbol. Certainly the bird must symbolize the soul, about to take off to its heavenly home.

The same bird-and-branches image is found on adults' stones, but not as the main image. See the base of the John Bishop stone (sandstone, 1785) (Fig. 116) Wolfville,[7] which has the characteristic Seaman cherub on the top. Similarly, the Isaac Deschamps stone (sandstone table, Windsor, 1805) (Fig. 117) shows a cherub in both upper corners around a bush with leaves and birds. The hatching on the bush has worn from flat exposure to rain, but the birds are the same as on the John Bishop and Edward Seaman stones. The bush has two drooping flowers (corporal remains) from which the birds (souls) are about to depart.

Thomas Lewis Seaman (1797-1890)
Abraham Seaman (1803-1880)

Thomas Lewis Seaman, son of Abraham Seaman, stayed in Kings County and was carving functional grave markers around Horton by 1840.[8] This seems a bit late in life to start, but there is so far little evidence of his work before then.

The Dr. Jacob Walton stone at Upper Canard (sandstone, 1840) (Fig. 118) is very plain except for two fine incised printer's dashes. T. L. Seaman wasn't thinking very far ahead when he used Sir Christopher Wren's epitaph, however. He carved "Si monumentum quaeris circumspice". (If you seek his monument look around you). Perhaps he had a grudge against Dr. Walton.

Thomas Lewis Seaman was listed as a marblecutter in New Minas, Kings County, along with his brother Abraham in 1864.[9] By 1866, Abraham appears to have teamed up with Henry B. Bishop and T.L. is listed as a farmer,[10] but in 1871 he is back in the game listed as a marble worker in New Minas.[11] His stones are marked "T.L.S./Horton" and are mainly plain or standard white stone. However, the Charles W. Harrison stone (white stone, 1867) marked "T.L.S." at Grand Pré (Fig 119) shows considerable skill in the carving. This is coated with lichen.

73

J. W. (c. 1820-1839)

J. W. stones are unique. Most J. W. stones are slate which possibly came from the slate quarry at Gore, Hants County. Because slate is brittle and flaky, gravestones made of this material tend to be short and almost squat. When you look at a number of photographs of J. W. stones there are few easily noticed characteristics which they have in common, and yet I can always spot them from a speeding car. This is because J. W. stones are not only slate — an uncommon material for the period — they are unusually tall and thin with oddly shaped shoulders. His stones are found in rural areas, particularly in many scattered locations in Hants County, with a number in the old parish burying ground in Windsor, one at Kentville and another at Upper Canard, Kings County (Fig. 120).

121

Although J. W. stones are found in community burial grounds with some church connection, his denominational affiliation is not certain. Perhaps this results from the jumble of ideas of people in a frontier situation who were prepared to listen to anyone purporting to be a minister, no matter what their own focus. The common denominator may have been the several Presbyterian variants. James Sprott, for instance, buried at Brooklyn, Hants County, with a J. W. stone, was the brother of John Sprott, missionary minister of the Church of Scotland, who worked all around the Newport circuit before moving on to Musquodoboit. John and Eleanor Clarke (two J. W. stones at Windsor) were John Sprott's first in-laws.[1]

No religious information is contained in J. W.'s use of symbols. He did use them, but poorly. In fact his symbols are so obscure as to be meaningless. He loved hairy faces, geometric squiggles, flat hands, coffin shapes, but these seem to have been used more for visual effect than to say anything. A lot of his wiggly lines may have been put in to fill up space, and these help obscure the image, whatever it is. His delight in lettering styles is much more obvious.

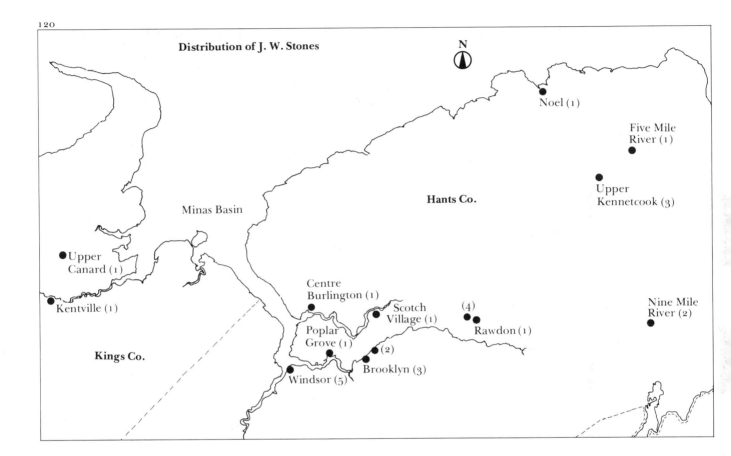

Distribution of J. W. Stones

N

Noel (1)

Five Mile
River (1)

Hants Co.

Upper
Kennetcook (3)

Minas Basin

Upper
Canard (1)

Centre
Burlington (1)

Nine Mile
River (2)

Scotch
Village (1)

(4)

Kentville (1)

Rawdon (1)

Poplar
Grove (1)

(2)

Kings Co.

Brooklyn (3)

Windsor (5)

Figure 122
Andrew Cummins, Kentville,
Kings Co.; slate, 1839.

Figure 123
James Robertson, Windsor,
Hants Co.; slate, 1837.

122

123

Figure 124
Samuel Murphy, Rawdon,
Hants Co.; slate, 1828.

124

The most noticeable characteristic of a J. W. stone is, of course, the very large "J. W. Sculptor" usually carved near the top. The information about the deceased is often bordered by some unusual geometric shape — frequently diamonds or circles. These also contain statements, or euphemisms, such as "Here Rest a clod of earth brighten into a star shining with all the radiant love of the Deity" (Fig. 123). The date is often obscured — added almost as an apology.

J. W.'s verses are invariably aimed at the reader. This is emphasized by some opening exhortation in capital letters: "Hark" or "Reader!" or, best of all, on the Shubael Dimock stone at Scotch Village, Hants County (slate, 1834) "Stand! All Hear! Read this!"

His common message to the reader is simple: "O look on this stone ye careless/trim your lamp and be sober". The moral lesson is that death is sudden and unexpected so you should clean up your act now and be ready for it. This is stated on each of his stones where he was given a free hand at expression.

How ought you on earth to live
While God prolongs the kind reprieve
And props the house of clay!
Your sole concern, your single care,
To watch, and tremble, and prepare
Against the fatal day!
Samuel Murphy, Rawdon, Hants County
(slate, 1828) (Fig. 124)

His number one favorite verse — the one he used most often — seems to be his own free verse, perhaps taken from a sermon which impressed him.

Life is uncertain
Tyrant death approaches
The Judge is at the door
Prepare to meet your God
Last Repentance being seldom sound
Ambrose Burton, Upper Kennetcook, Hants County
(slate, 1832)

Figure 125
(a) John MaDill, Rawdon, Hants
Co.; slate, 1830
(b) Top detail

This last line varies. See, for instance, the John MaDill stone at Rawdon, Hants County (slate, 1830) (Fig. 125) where he added:

If you love to die well
Take care to live better.

Teetering on the brink of death was one of his choice images:

Here pause a while
For here we all must lie
Infinite joy or endless woe
Attend on every breath
And yet how unconcern'd we go
Upon the brink of death
Prepare to meet thy God.
McPhee children, Nine Mile River, Hants County (slate, 1829) (Fig. 126)

Again:

Stop poor sinner, stop and think
Before you farther go;
Will you sport upon the brink
Of everlasting woe!
Robert O'Brien, Noel, Hants County (slate, 1833)

The oldest signed J. W. stone is at Poplar Grove, Hants County, on the way to Newport Landing. This is in a family plot on private land in a little gully, and commemorates Sarah Smith, who died in 1814 (Fig. 127), but was probably carved later, perhaps in 1820 when the second Mrs. Smith, another Sarah, died (Fig. 128). The Sarah Smith stone, signed J. W., is sandstone, not slate. It is very subdued when compared with his later work. The geometric squiggles and drapery are already present, as is a small hairy face — all characteristics of his later work.

The Daniel Weir stone, Rawdon, Hants County (sandstone, 1825) (Fig. 129) is perhaps the next in the chronology of J. W. stones I have seen.[1] This is also

78

125a

125b

Figure 126
Cameron/William McPhee, Nine Mile River, Hants Co.; slate, 1828.

Figure 127
Sarah Smith, Poplar Grove, Hants Co.; sandstone, 1814.

Figure 128
Sarah Smith, Poplar Grove, Hants Co.; sandstone, 1820.

Figure 129
Daniel Wier, Rawdon, Hants Co., sandstone; 1825.

128

126

129

127

subdued and the verse is an old standard; however, the lettering variations give J. W. away.

J. W. worked for visual effect, in my opinion. The massive size, the ornate shapes and borders and elaborate lettering were all calculated to impress the viewer. After all, he was dealing with a still largely illiterate population. Although his verses, comments and symbols don't always make sense, his stones are definitely awe-inspiring.

In the Hants County probate records there is no clue as to who was being paid to carve gravestones. The people the stones commemorate appear to have died fairly affluent farmers, yet at the end of their long and involved wills we find marks, instead of signatures, made by hands obviously unaccustomed to holding anything as fine as a pen. To those who paid J. W. to carve stones, they must have seemed very fine memorials indeed. They are.

J. W.'s name should be James Wood. This is pure conjecture on my part — there seems to be no traceable reference to his identity. There was a James Wood, Junior, stonecarver at Windsor, whose period of carving activity works out to be in the generation after J. W. His use of the term "Junior" seems to imply there was a Senior in the same business. Other gravestone carvers with the surname Wood were working in the next generation in the Halifax area, although their relationship to James Wood, Junior is not known.

The only evidence, if you can call it that, is a note by Harry Piers (1870-1940) in his personal copy of a paper read before the Nova Scotia Historical Society in 1932. Beside a reference to a stone marked "J. W. Sculptor", Piers wrote in the margin "Wood of Hfx".[2]

Judging by the dispersal of J. W. stones, it is more probable that J. W. worked out of Windsor. Whoever he was, his work is unique and fascinating.

Coll Campbell

Figure 130
Allan McKinnon, Strathlorne,
Inverness Co.; white stone, 1897.

Figure 131
Donald McKinnon, Strathlorne,
Inverness Co.; white stone, 1901.

Another folksy carver, Coll Campbell, worked more recently in white stone. His work is found in Inverness County, particularly at Strathlorne, and was done circa 1897-1902. Coll Campbell stones are massive pieces of white stone covered with imagery. When viewed through gathering dusk their unusual outlines resemble looming white human figures.

Coll Campbell particularly liked a central image of the last handshake, with a willow tree on either shoulder, and perhaps a cluster of grapes on a vine or a peculiar branch with rose (?) blossoms sprouting from the handshake.

Notice on the Allan McKinnon stone, Strathlorne, Inverness County, 1897, (Fig. 130) the attempts at ornate lettering, the last minute addition of "OF" at the top, and particularly the awkward positioning of the hands. Coll Campbell appears to have been a "folk artist", working outside the mainstream of popular gravestone design.

130

131

Stonecarvers and Marble Works in Nova Scotia

This listing should not be regarded as complete. The dates given are for the period in which carving was done, and in most cases have been taken from actual stones; thus there may have been stones made at a later period and back dated, or dates may have been added later; or companies may have continued under a different name. There is a very good chance that there are many carvers whose advertisements or marks have not yet been discovered.

A., D. & Co., c. 1843-1851
    Windsor, N.S.

Adams & Co., c. 1850-1851
    Windsor, N.S.

Adams & Drake, c. 1850-1852
    Windsor, N.S.

Amherst Granite and Marble Works, c. 1907-1914

Andres, A. W., c. 1845-1853
    Dorchester, N.B.

Andres, Stephen Baker, c. 1862-1889
    Amherst, N.S.

Andres & Tomas, (no data)

Archer, Joseph Tupper, c. 1849 (d. 1863, aged 81)
    Yarmouth, N.S.

Arsenault Monumental Works Ltd., c.1976
    Antigonish, N.S.

Bardsley, R., c. 1892
    Brussels St. opp. Clarence St.,
    Saint John, N.B.

Barton, George, c. 1832 (see also Daly & Barton)
    adjoining Cunard's stone store,
    Halifax, N.S.

Baxter, G.B., c. 1888-1889
    Fredericton, N.B.

Beaton, c. 1914 (see MacDonald & Beaton)

Bishop Hx. (see William Bishop)
    Halifax, N.S.

Bishop, Fredericton E., c. 1918-1922
    Halifax, N.S.

Bishop, H. & L., c. 1856-1863
    Horton, N.S.

Bishop, Henry, c. 1842-1859 (see also H. & L. Bishop)
    Horton, N.S.

Bishop, Lucius B., c. 1871-1873 (see also H. & L. Bishop)
    Horton, N.S.

Bishop, William, c. 1874-1920 (see also Bishop & Evans and Halifax Marble Works)
    Halifax, N.S.
    corner of Barrington and Blowers Sts. (1876)
    16 and 18 Barrington St. (1877)
    73 and 75 Barrington St. (1884)
    73 and 75 Barrington St. (1897)
    Wm. Bishop and Son, 51-53 Sackville St. (1908)

Bishop & A. Seaman, c. 1860-1869
    Horton, N.S.

Bishop & Evans, c. 1865-1873
    (see also Halifax Marble Works)
    Halifax, N.S.

Botick, H., c. 1848

Brush (see Lambert & Brush)

Brush, Alfred, c. 1863-1865
    Yarmouth, N.S.

Campbell, Coll, c. 1897-1901
    (d. 1925) Inverness Co., N.S.

Charman, Henry C., c. 1886-1914
    Wallace, N.S.

Clare, J.P., c. 1863

Clarey Bros., c. 1932
    Stellarton, N.S.

Clear, F. W., c. 1850-1864
    Canning and Berwick, Kings Co., N.S.

Coughlan Granite and Marble Works
　　Halifax, N.S., c. 1907 to present
　　1 Connolly St., c. 1907
　　189 Chebucto Rd., 1936, 1937
　　located on North West Arm and also at Simpson's
　　Siding for a time
　　31 Bedford Highway (James S. Coughlan and Sons)
　　c. 1968-1973; sold to Smith Brothers of Montreal,
　　1973, but retained the name T.D. Coughlan and
　　Sons. Advertisement states "est. 1821" but this is not
　　substantiated.

Cox, Sidney B., c. 1904-1943
　　Truro, N.S.

Craven, H., c. 1842-1847
　　Halifax, N.S. (?)

Crook, D. E., c. 1898-1908
　　Sydney, N.S.

Daly & Barton, c. 1828-1832
　　Halifax, N.S.

Daly, Charles (see Daly & Barton)

Dares, D., c. 1776

Dartmouth Granite and Marble Works (Rufus H.
　　MacLeod), c. 1938-1956

Dauphinee, A.T., 1908-1933
　　Shelburne, N.S. (moved the business to Yarmouth)

Dauphinee, W.T., Ltd. (Wilfred Tennyson), 1933 to
　　the present
　　Shelburne, N.S.

Davis, R., c. 1858
　　Halifax, N.S.
　　Water St. cor. North St.

Dearness, John (son of Thomas), c. 1898-1900
　　Bridgetown, N.S.

Dearness, Thomas, c. 1860-1873
　　Saint John, N.B.
　　(bought Falconer & Whitman in Bridgetown, N.S.
　　c. 1887-1898) (d. 1898)

Delaney, Ed., c. 1863

DeMone, Cyril
　　Lunenburg, N.S. still in operation, finishing and
　　lettering

Dewar, A. S., c. 1908
　　Wallace, N.S.

Dillou, J., c. 1844

Donoghue, S., c. 1848-1863

Drake (see Adams & Drake)

Drake, James H. (Fig. 132), c. 1855-1856
　　Halifax, N.S.
　　Hollis St.

Drysdale (see Sutherland & Drysdale)

Drysdale, Arthur J., c. 1870-1890
　　Bridgewater, N.S.

Drysdale & Hoyt Bros., c. 1871-1885
　　Bridgetown, N.S.
　　(This was Arthur J. Drysdale, who with Jesse Hoyt
　　was in Bridgetown in 1884)

Evans (see Bishop & Evans)

Evans, A.K., c. 1887

Evans, James A., c. 1870-1876 (see also Bishop & Evans,
　　Halifax Marble Works)
　　Halifax, N.S.
　　73 and 75 Barrington St.

Falconer & Whitman, c. 1878-1887
　　(Daniel Falconer & Oldham Whitman)
　　Bridgetown, N.S.

Faulkner, W. H., c. 1883-1888
　　(two dimensional cast iron markers)

Fitzgerald, c. 1840-1867
　　Saint John, N.B.

Fitzgerald & McKim, c. 1850
　　Saint John, N.B.

Foote, (no data)

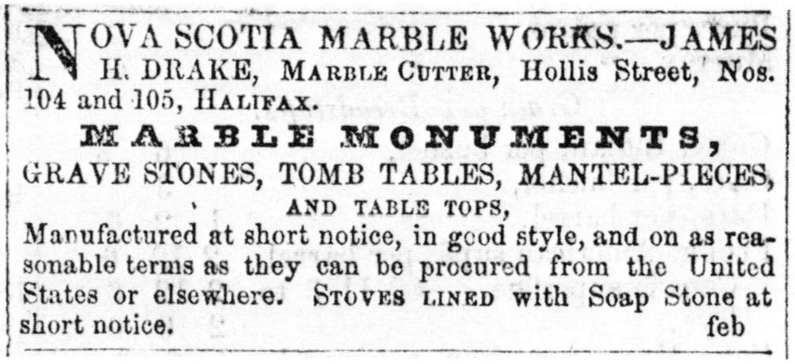

Figure 132
Advertisement for James Drake in the
Halifax Atheneum, *October 11,
1855. (Photo by R. Merrick)*

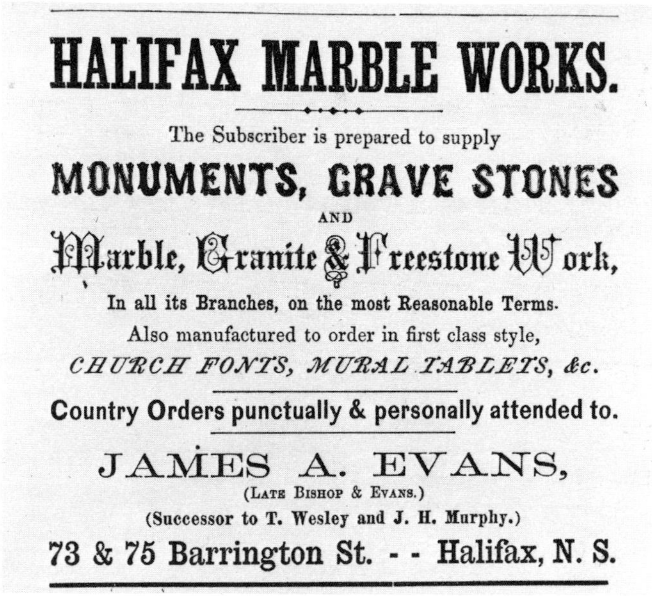

Figure 133
Advertisement for Halifax Marble
Works in *McAlpine's Halifax
Directory, 1871.
(Photo by R. Merrick)*

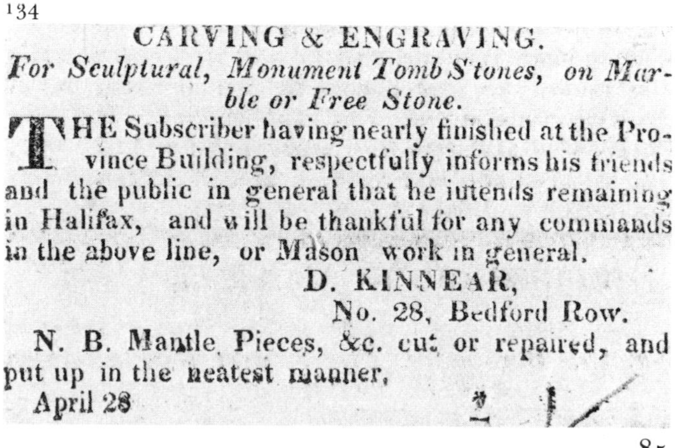

Figure 134
Advertisement for David Kinnear in
the Halifax Free Press, *April 1818.
(Photo by R. Merrick)*

Foote & Wood, c. 1863
  Halifax, N.S. (?)

Fox (*see* Walker & Fox)

Fox, R. L., c. 1860-1877
  Truro, N.S.
  Also in Moncton 1877

Fredericton Steam Marble Works, c. 1880-1911
  (John Moore & Sons)

Gauan, P., c. 1845

Goudey, R. H., c. 1917
  Horton St., Yarmouth, N.S.
  Successor to J. H. McGill & Co.

Gray, Henry C. (Gray's Monument Works), c. 1970
  617 Windmill Rd., Dartmouth, N.S.

Gray, William F., c. 1897-1938
  108 Gerrish St., Halifax, N.S.

Griffin & Keltie
  Halifax, N.S. c. 1873-1927 (established 1873)
  244 Barrington St. (1884)
  323-325 Barrington St. (1892-1911)
  687-689 Barrington St. (1918-1922)
  When Michael Griffin died in 1898 Robert Keltie
  ran the business himself. On his death Robert Keltie
  Jr. changed the name to Robert Keltie & Son.

Griffin, Michael J., c. 1873-1877 (d. 1898)
  Halifax, N.S.

Hagan, c. 1872

Halifax Marble Works (Fig. 133), 1862-c.1900

Hamill, O. (archt.) with J. H. Johnstone, cutter, c.
1862-1865

Hanson (*see* Walker & Hanson)

Hanson, John F., c. 1908
  Kentville, N.S.

132

NOVA SCOTIA MARBLE WORKS.—JAMES
H. DRAKE, MARBLE CUTTER, Hollis Street, Nos.
104 *and* 105, HALIFAX.
MARBLE MONUMENTS,
GRAVE STONES, TOMB TABLES, MANTEL-PIECES,
AND TABLE TOPS,
Manufactured at short notice, in good style, and on as rea-
sonable terms as they can be procured from the United
States or elsewhere. STOVES LINED with Soap Stone at
short notice.   feb

133

HALIFAX MARBLE WORKS.

The Subscriber is prepared to supply

MONUMENTS, GRAVE STONES

AND

Marble, Granite & Freestone Work,

In all its Branches, on the most Reasonable Terms.
Also manufactured to order in first class style,
CHURCH FONTS, MURAL TABLETS, &c.

Country Orders punctually & personally attended to.

JAMES A. EVANS,
(LATE BISHOP & EVANS.)
(Successor to T. Wesley and J. H. Murphy.)

73 & 75 Barrington St. - - Halifax, N. S.

134

CARVING & ENGRAVING.
*For Sculptural, Monument Tomb Stones, on Mar-
ble or Free Stone.*
THE Subscriber having nearly finished at the Province Building, respectfully informs his friends
and the public in general that he intends remaining
in Halifax, and will be thankful for any commands
in the above line, or Mason work in general.
                                    D. KINNEAR,
                              No. 28, Bedford Row.
  N. B. Mantle Pieces, &c. cut or repaired, and
put up in the neatest manner.
April 28

Figure 135
Advertisement for Morrison Brothers, Pictou, in McAlpine's Gazetteer of Nova Scotia, New Brunswick, Prince Edward Island and Newfoundland, 1911. (Photo by R. Merrick)

Figure 136
Advertisement for J.H. Murphy's Marble Works in Hutchinson's Halifax Directory, 1863. (Photo by R. Merrick)

Figure 137
Advertisement for Richard Scott in the Acadian Recorder, April 1819. Remsheg was an early name for Wallace, Cumberland Co., N.S. (Courtesy Public Archives of Nova Scotia. Photo by R. Merrick)

135

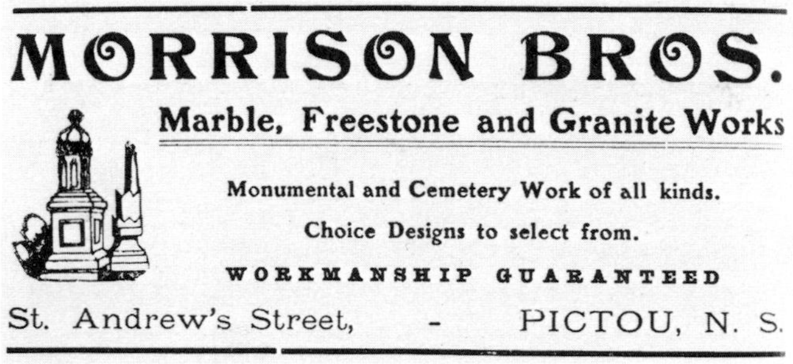

136

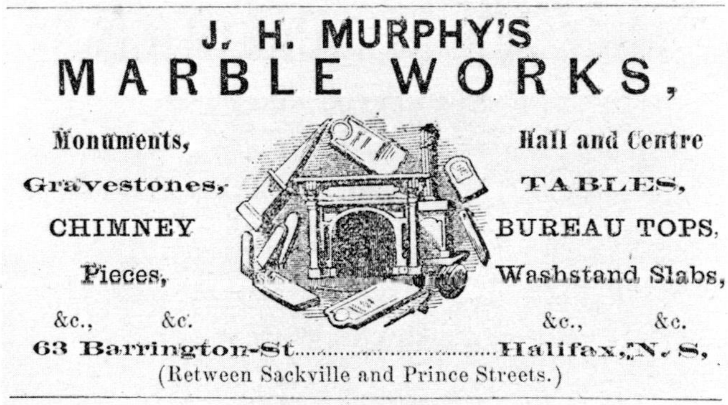

137

Harpell, Alonzo B., c. 1922-1956
  Halifax, N.S.
  141 Upper Water St. (1922)
  702 1/2 Robie St. (1927)
  94 1/2 Windsor St. (1937-1956)

Harvey, B. W., c. 1866

Hattie, G., c. 1828-1840
  Pictou Co. (?)

Hay, James, c. 1775-1793
  Halifax, N.S.
  (From Scotland)
  Father of John Hay

Hay, James W., c. 1833-1843
  Son of Peter Hay
  Halifax, N.S.

Hay, John, c. 1792-1820
  Halifax, N.S.

Hay, Peter, c. 1812-1832 (d. 1832)
  Halifax, N.S.
  Although he died in 1832 there are stones signed by him in Parrsboro and Lunenburg dated 1836.

Henderson (see McNutt & Henderson)

Henderson, A., c. 1913-1916
  Truro, N.S.

Henderson, John & Son, c. 1812
  Halifax, N.S.

Heritage Memorials, in N.B. from 1909 and in N.S. from 1967.
  Still in operation (1978)
  Windsor, N.S

Holmes, James, c. 1866-1867
  Yarmouth, N.S.

Hopkins, G., c. 1864
  Antigonish, N.S.

Hoyt, Jesse W. (see Drysdale & Hoyt Bros.)

Hoyt Bros. (Jesse and Arthur) late 1880's
  Bridgetown, N.S.

Hoyt, W. J. & Son, c. 1908
    Bridgetown, N.S.
    Jesse and son Charles

Hoyt & Reed, (Middleton Marble Works), c. 1911-1914
    Middleton, N.S.
    Charles M. Hoyt & A. M. Reed

Hunter, c. 1862
    Baie Verte, N.B.

Hunter, E.G., c. 1884

Hutchison, D., c. 1889-1903
    Baddeck, N.S.

Johnstone, John H., c. 1858-1865
    Halifax, N.S.

Judge, Thomas S., (Liverpool Marble Works),
    c. 1891-1914
    Liverpool, N.S.

Kane & Co., c. 1867-1892
    Saint John, N.B.
    Waterloo St.

Keddy, C. L., (Keddy Monument Works), c. 1936-1956
    171-173 Kempt Rd., Halifax, N.S.

Kelly, George J., c. 1877-1934
    Bridgewater, N.S.

Keltie (see Griffin & Keltie)

Keltie, Robert & Son, c. 1927-1971
    Halifax, N.S.
    687 Barrington St. (1936-1938)
    39 Yukon St. (1947-1956)
    6317 Yukon St. (1964-1971)

Kentville Marble Works, c. 1908

King, James, c. 1868-1895 (d. 1910)
    Halifax and New Glasgow

Kinnear, David (Fig. 134), c. 1818-1821
    Halifax, N.S.

Kinsella, A., c. 1884-1904
    Saint John, N.B.

Kinsop, R., c. 1824
    Saint John, N.B.

Kline, John Jr., (Kline's Granite & Monument Works),
    c. 1877-1918
    Halifax, N.S.

Lambert, J. A., c. 1833-1862
    Yarmouth, N.S.

Lambert & Brush, c. 1855-1863
    Yarmouth, N.S.

Lang, George, c. 1860-1865
    Halifax, N.S.

Lowden, B. L., c. 1898-1908
    Probably Cape Breton

M., A., c. 1888

Liverpool Marble Works (see T. S. Judge)

M., H.J., c. 1861

Malcolm & Turnbull, c. 1833
    Halifax, N.S.

Mahar, Michael J., c. 1880-1900
    75 Grafton St., Halifax, N.S.
    (Chebucto Marble Works, 1884)

Maritime Monument Works, (H. G. Newcomb
    & H. W. Tingley), c. 1927
    171-173 Kempt Rd., Halifax, N.S.

McAdam, James Chipman (Amherst Granite and
    Marble Works), c. 1907-1914
    Amherst, N.S.

M. C. & J., c. 1859

McDonald, R., c. 1875
    Pictou, N.S.

McDonald & Beaton, c. 1914
    Sydney, N.S.

McEachern
    Halifax, N.S. (?) n.d.

McGill, Joseph & Co., c. 1907-1914
  Yarmouth, N.S.

McGill, Oliver, c. 1865-1908(*see also* Yarmouth Marble Works)
  Yarmouth, N.S.

McGowan, c. 1861-1863 (*see also* Thomas & McGowan)

McGrath, H.J., c. 1868-1871
  Saint John, N.B.

McGrattan, H. & Sons, Marble & Granite Works, c. 1923
  Sydney, N.S.
  384 George St.

McIsaac, John, c. 1872-1905
  St. Andrews, Antigonish Co., N.S.

McKenzie, W. R., c. 1879-1902
  Archimedes St., New Glasgow, N.S.

MacKenzie & Scott, c. 1875-1876

McKim, c. 1855 (*see also* Fitzgerald & McKim)

MacKim, Robert A., c. 1868-1887
  273 Gower St., St. John's, Nfld.

McLellan, R.
  c. 1866-1869

McLeod, John J., c. 1908
  Lower Stewiacke

MacLeod, Rufus H., Dartmouth
  Granite & Marble Works, c. 1938-1956
  125 Ochterloney St., Dartmouth, N.S.
  (MacLeod's Monument Works)
  50 Canal St., 1964 to the present

McNutt & Henderson, c. 1910-1915
  Truro, N.S.

McNutt, F. B., c. 1899-1947
  Truro, N.S.

McP., A (?), c. 1884-1896
  New Glasgow, N.S.

McPherson, John, c. 1858-1886
  New Glasgow, N.S.

Middleton Granite & Marble Co., c. 1911-1914
  (*see also* Hoyt & Reed)

Miller, A., c. 1866-1884
  Queen St., Truro, N.S.

Milligan, J. & R., c. 1850-1882
  Saint John, N.B.
  King Square near Sydney

Milligan, Robert, c. 1892
  Saint John, N.B.

Moore, John & Sons, c. 1880-1911
  (*see* Fredericton Steam Marble Works)

Morrison, c. 1835-1840
  Pictou, N.S.

Morrison Bros., (Fig. 135) c. 1885-1914
  Pictou, N.S.

Morrison, J. W., c. 1865-1884
  Pictou, N.S.

Morrison, Murdoch, c. 1865-1869
  Pictou, N.S.

Murphy (*see* Seaman & Murphy)

Murphy, James H., (Fig. 136) c. 1855-1885
  Halifax, N.S.
  Spring Garden Rd. near Queen St. (1859)
  63 Barrington St. between Sackville & Prince (1863 onward)

Myatt, Albert H., c. 1908
  Oxford, N.S.

N., T., c. 1827

Newcomb, H.G. (*see* Maritime Monument Works),
  c. 1927

Nicholson, A. R., c. 1893
  Cape Breton (?)

Nixon, A. & R., (Nixon Granite Works Ltd.), c. 1976
  Nictaux Falls, Annapolis Co.

Osgood, S. P., c. 1848-1886
King St., Saint John, N.B.
Osgood's seems to have been a very popular
company through the 1850's and early 1860's in
Nova Scotia. From 1848-1858 he drove his own
team through N.B. and N.S., working up a large
business.

Page, J. M. & Son, c. 1889-1890
Truro, N.S.

Page (see Walker & Page)

Philip, H.C., c. 1878-1881
Saint John, N.B.

Purvis, James, c. 1892-1920
Windsor, N.S.

Raymond (see Walker & Raymond)

Raymond, Samuel F., c. 1861-1865 (d. 1872)
Main near Central St., Yarmouth, N.S.
Was also in partnership with O. McGill (see also
Yarmouth Monument Works)

Rice, Thelbert
Bear River, Digby Co.
1895-1921, when plant was moved to Nictaux West,
Annapolis Co., the site of their granite quarries. (d.
1935) (Information from W. D. Rice, Dec., 1976)

Rice, Willis D.
Nictaux West, Annapolis Co. 1921-1928
Moved finishing plant to Middleton, 1928-1946.
Sold to W. T. Scott, 1946; retained quarries at
Nictaux West.

Reed (see Hoyt & Reed)

Rose, W., c. 1866
New Glasgow, N.S.

Ross, Charles A., c. 1895-1914
New Glasgow, N.S.

Rottler, A. A., c. 1914
Kentville, N.S.

S. & McG. (Steel & McGrattan?), c. 1902
North Sydney, N.S.

Sanford (see Wesley & Sanford)

Sanford, Frederick, c. 1884-1938
Halifax, N.S.
Son of George A. Sanford

Sanford, George A. (& Sons)
Halifax, N.S. (Established 1860)
12 Barrington St. (1866-1867)
82-86 Argyle St. (1876-1886)
82-84 Argyle St. (1892-1938)
82 Argyle St. (1936-1940)

Sanford, Harry B., c. 1884-1938
Halifax, N.S.
Son of George A. Sanford

Saunders, S., c. 1858
1 Brunswick St., Halifax, N.S.

Scott (see MacKenzie & Scott)

Scott, Richard, (Fig. 137), c. 1819 (d. 1867)
Wallace and Halifax

Seaman, Abraham, c. 1812-1821 (b. 1767-d. 1848)
Horton and Cumberland.
Father of Thomas Lewis Seaman and Abraham
Seaman

Seaman, Abraham, c. 1864-1871 (b. 1803-d. 1880)
(see also Bishop and A. Seaman)
Horton/New Minas, Kings Co.
Son of Abraham. Married Nancy R. Allison, 1834

Seaman, Thomas Lewis, c. 1858-1883 (b. 1797-d.
1890)
Horton/New Minas, Kings Co.
Son of Abraham

Seaman, Lewis, c. 1843
Horton, Kings Co.
(Is this "T.L."?)

Seaman & Murphy, c. 1846-1858
Horton, Kings Co.

Seaton, J. S., c. 1875-1886

Sharp, D., c. 1923-1936
   New Glasgow, N.S.
   (From Scotland 1910 to Colonial Granite Works,
   New Glasgow. Established own business 1923)

Shaw, D., c. 1804
   Amherst, N.S.

Shelburne Granite and Marble Works, c. 1914-1924
   (C. G. Reed, manager)

Sherman, Edward, c. 1866-1867
   Yarmouth, N.S.

Sherrard, c. 1941

Sherrard, F. F. & Co., c. 1870
   Point du Chene, N.B.

Sinclair (see Wesley & Sinclair)

Sinclair, J., c. 1854
   Halifax, N.S.

Sleeth, W., c. 1845-1846
   Saint John, N.B.

Sleeth & Barber, c. 1847
   Saint John, N.B.

Smith, J. P., (from England), c. 1834-1847
   Windsor, N.S.

Smith, H. E., c. 1857-1891
   Pictou, N.S.

Smith Bros. Granite Ltd., c. 1976
   Halifax, N.S.

Steele, John D. & Co. Granite & Marble Works
   c. 1889 to present
   North Sydney, N.S.

Stewart, James, c. 1839-1842
   Pictou Co.

Sutherland & Drysdale, c. 1876-1882
   Kentville, N.S.

Sydney Marble Works, c. 1889

Tantallon Monument Works,
   Smith, 1959-1972
   C. F. Snelgrove, 1972 to present.

Tay, William, c. 1868-1869
   56 Duke St., Saint John, N.B.

Thomas, R. B., n.d.
   Dorchester, N.B.

Thomas & Macgowan, c. 1859
   Dorchester, N.B. (?)

Thomson, John, c. 1785-1789
   Shelburne, N.S.

Tingley Monuments (Fig. 138)
   Cape Hopewell, N.B.
   Founded 1846 by John C. Tingley; taken over by his
   son, J. Alton Tingley, 1888; moved operation to
   Amherst 1919; still in operation (1978) by fifth
   generation of the Tingley family.

Tingley, Harold W. (Maritime Monument Works)
   c. 1927-1956
   Halifax, N.S.
   Merkel St. (from 1936 on)
   Son of J. A. Tingley
   (Information supplied by D. W. Tingley)

Tomas (see Andres & Tomas)

Truro Monument Works, c. 1971
   Truro, N.S.
   Still in operation

Treen, J., c. 1883
   New Glasgow, N.S.

Turnbull (see Malcolm & Turnbull)

W. J., c. 1816-1839
   Hants Co.

Walker, Albert J. (Fig. 139)
   Truro, N.S., Established 1857
   (d. 1920, aged 85)

138

139

140

NEW ADVERTISEMENTS.

STONE CUTTING, &c.

WILLIAM WOOD, in returning thanks for past favours, begs to acquaint the Gentry and Public, generally, of Halifax and the Province of Nova-Scotia, that he continues to execute the above business, at the head of the Long Wharf—and all orders left at his Workshop, or at his Residence, No 99, Granville street, for HEAD OR TOMB STONES, &c. Shall be executed in a style of Workmanship, equal to any imported and superior to any of the kind in Halifax and upon as reasonable terms.

N. B.—The Subscriber begs to intimate that he has no connection in business with any other person whatever, and to prevent false impressions all work in the above line, executed by him shall be marked with W. Wood, *Sculpt.*

August 11.   Tiew Post.

141

Walker, Lyman J., c. 1857-1926
    Truro, N.S.
    Son of A. J. Walker

Walker, J. A., c. 1882-1886
    Antigonish, N.S.

Walker & Co., c. 1872-1885
    Kentville, N.S.

Walter & Fox, c. 1871-1875
    Truro, N.S.

Walker & Hanson, c. 1865-1884
    Kentville, N.S.

Walker & Page, c. 1873-1886
    Truro, N.S.

Walker & Raymond, c. 1850-1861
    Yarmouth, N.S.

Walker & Son
    Truro, N.S. (A.J. and L. J. Walker)

Wesley, Thomas, c. 1848-1868 (*see also* Halifax Marble
    Works)
    Halifax, N.S.

Wesley and Sanford (*see also* Halifax Marble Works)
    Halifax, N.S. c. 1860-1867
    Established 1852

Wesley and Sinclair, c. 1847-1852
    Halifax, N.S.

Whitman, (*see* Falconer & Whitman)
    Whitman, Oldham, c. 1882-1916
    Bridgetown, N.S.

Wilton, R. T., c. 1865
    Glace Bay, N.S.

Wood (*see* Foote & Wood)

Wood, Andrew, c. 1866-1871
    Halifax, N.S.,
    Son of James & Ellen Wood

Wood, James Jr., (Fig. 141), c. 1843-1874
    Stannus St., Windsor, N.S.

Wood, Thomas Stone, c. 1862-1897
    Stannus St., Windsor, N.S.

Wood, William, (Fig. 140), c. 1845-1864
    Halifax, N.S.

Yarmouth Marble Works, c. 1861-1917 (*see also* S. F.
    Raymond, O. McGill, J. McGill)
    Yarmouth, N.S.

Foreign Carvers Whose Work is Found in Nova Scotia

Cary, A., c. 1837-1854
  Boston, Mass.

Chantrey, c. 1817
  London, England

?, c. 1816
  Charlestown Mass.

Codner, Abraham, c. 1774
  "Next the DrawBridge Boston"

Dares, D., c. 1776

Ealms (?) Olver, c. 1819
  (signature chipped)

Gibson, I.
  Romae

Jones & Willis, c. 1890

Kimball, Chester, c. 1785
  N. London, Conn.

Knapp, J. H., c. 1830-1839
  Foley St., London

Maxcy, L., c. 1793
  Salem, Mass.

Nixon, c. 1835-1840

Physick, R., c. 1851-2
  King St. — St. James, London

Piper & Son, c. 1803
  London

Seddon, G. M., c. 1841
  Liverpool (England)

Wood, L. E., c. 1815-1823
  Chelsea, London

Woodington, W. F., c. 1827-1839
  London

Notes

The First Cut

1 Von Franz, M.L., "The Process of Individuation" in *Man and his Symbols,* ed. by Carl G. Jung. New York, Doubleday, 1964, pp. 221-224.

2 This was actually doctrinally established by St. Thomas Aquinas, St. Augustine and other influential theologians. The Council of Trent, in 1563, affirmed that relic veneration was permitted.

3 Burgess, Frederick, *English Churchyard Memorials.* London, Lutterworth Press, 1963, p. 20.

4 For more comprehensive information on New England traditions, see: Forbes, Harriet Merrifield, *Gravestones of Early New England and the Men who made Them 1653-1800.* Boston, Houghton Mifflin, 1927. Also see Ludwig, Allan I., *Graven Images.* Middletown, Conn., Wesleyan University Press, 1966.

French and Indians

1 Blackman, Margaret B., "Mortuary Art from the Northwest Coast", *The Beaver,* Winter 1975, pp. 54-57. Also Veilette, John and White, Gary, *Early Indian Village Churches; Wooden Frontier Architecture in British Columbia.* Vancouver, University of British Columbia Press, 1977.

2 McLeod, Robert R., *Markland or Nova Scotia; its History, Natural Resources and Native Beauties.* Toronto, J.L. Nichols Co. Ltd., 1902, p.171.

For further information see: Gilpin, J. Bernard, "On the Stone Age of Nova Scotia." *Proceedings & Transactions of the N.S. Institute of Natural Science,* V.3, 1874, p. 227.

3 Patterson, George, *Memoirs of the Rev. James MacGregor D. D.,* Philadelphia, Joseph M. Wilson, 1859, p. 263, in a description of French remains at Waugh's River, Pictou Co., about 1790 mentions "Traces also of a graveyard, with the cross still standing at the head of the graves."

Imported Stones of the Eighteenth Century

1 Attributed to Nathaniel Emmes, Boston, active c. 1717-1750.

2 Hartz, Lewis, *The Founding of New Societies.* New York, Harcourt, Brace, 1964.

3 A cherub, by definition, is near the bottom in angel hierarchy. Cherubim are "images of men with wings and comely faces": Tashjian, Dickran and Ann, *Memorials for Children of Change,* Middletown, Conn., Wesleyan University Press, 1974, pp. 83-84 from a definition of 1661. Thus a cherub is not necessarily a Cupid-like figure.

4 Compare with Rev. Shear Jashub Bourne stone, 1768, Roxbury, Mass. (Ludwig, *op. cit.,* plate 178) Codner was sending elaborate stone to Charleston, South Carolina, about the same period. (See Ravenel, Beatrice St. J., "Here Lyes Buried, Taste and Trade in Charleston Tombstones", *Antiques,* March, 1942, v. 41, no. 3, pp. 193-195.)

5 For further information on Chester Kimball, see Caulfield, Ernest. "Connecticut Gravestones, XIII," continued by Peter Benes, *Connecticut Historical Society Bulletin,* April 1975, Vol. 40 No. 2, pp. 36-38.

Angel Heads

1 The topic is discussed at length by A. I. Ludwig, *Graven Images* and by Dickran and Ann Tashjian, *Memorials for Children of Change.*

2 Ludwig, *op. cit.,* pp. 223-225

3 *Ibid, p.* 283.

4 *Ibid.,* p. 274.

5 Wither, George, *A Collection of Emblemes Ancient and Moderne* Columbia, S.C., University of South Carolina Press, 1975. (Reprint of 1635 edition) Illus. XVIII; Bk. 3.

6 Quarles, Frances, *Hieroglyphikes* (1638). Reprinted by Scolar Press, 1975, pp. 18-19, Hierogliph V.

7 Tashjian, *op. cit.,* p. 84.

Primitive Local Carving

1 Richardson, Evelyn M., "Barrington's Old Meeting House". Reprinted from *The Advertiser,* Kentville, (Blossom edition) May 1968, p. 5. "Few of these [graves of the first settlers] had been marked by more than wooden pieces, and by 1838 no memory of most remained."

2 Local tradition has it that the Jannet McDonald buried here was somehow related to Flora McDonald of Bonnie Prince Charlie fame. It is said that Jannet was buried in the sheets in which the Prince slept while on the run after the battle of Culloden.

3 IHS from the first three letters of the Greek word meaning Jesus.

The Second Horton Carver

1 Other stones from the first period: in Upper Canard - Eliza Wells (1800), Joseph Chase (1801); in Chipman's Corner - Charlotte Curry (1799), Handley Chipman (1799), Jane Chipman (1775 - this is probably a case of backdating. The stone may have been carved at the same time as that for Handley); in Wolfville - Nathan Rand (1801), Lucretia Rogers (1801); in Kentville - Benjamin Peck (1801).

2 Other stones from the second period: in Upper Canard - Eunice Harris (1803), Perry Borden Senior (1805), Martha Harris (1802); in Chipman's Corner - Nancy Chipman (1802), Stephen Post (1768 - this must have been backdated); in Wolfville - Gilbert Forsyth (1802), Mary Forsyth (1796 - again probably carved at the same time as her husband's), James Duncanson (1802), Ann Bishop (1803), Carolina Bishop (1803), Samuel Reed (1805); between Wolfville and Melanson on Maple St. - Anna Fitch (1802), Lydia Fitch (1797 - again a probable case of backdating); in West Amherst - William Freeman (1801). How this got to West Amherst is a good question.

The Annapolis Carver

1 The probate records of Annapolis County, as recorded on microfilm at the Public Archives of Nova Scotia, are meagre indeed, with large portions missing. Digby County probate records are indexed, but there are no papers at Halifax beyond the index. Thus the Annapolis carver remains unidentified.

German Stones

1 There is an interesting similarity between German gravestones in Nova Scotia and German stones in Southwest Virginia. For comparison see Wust, Klaus, *Folk Art in Stone.* Edinburg, Virginia. Shenandoah History, 1970.

2 Translation by Niels Jannasch. Wilhelmsfeld is a few miles northeast of Heidelberg.

Trumpeting Figures

1 Will of Handley Chipman (cabinetmaker by trade), 1799. P.A.N.S. Estate papers, Kings County, N.S.

Willow and Urn

1 Keese, John, ed., *The Floral Keepsake,* N.Y., Leavitt and Allen, n.d. [c. 1850] p. 106.

2 Ferguson, George, *Dictionary of Christian Symbols,* N.Y., 1961, p.40.

3 For data on the frequency of willow and urn images over time in Massachusetts, see Edwin Dethlefsen and James Deetz, "Death's Heads, Cherubs, and Willow Trees: Experimental Archaeology in Colonial Cemeteries" *American Antiquity* v. 31 no. 4 (April 1966) pp. 502-510. Also James Deetz and Edwin S. Dethlefsen, "Death's Head Cherub Urn and Willow" *Natural History* v. 76 no. 3 (March 1967) pp. 28-37.

4 This is blatant generalization on my part. Actually, the evidence is in the gravestones, or rather, the lack of them.

The Rural Cemetery Movement

1 Bender, Thomas, "The 'Rural' Cemetery Movement: Urban Travail and the Appeal of Nature", *New England Quarterly,* v. XLVII, no. 2, June, 1974, pp. 196-211.

2 French, Stanley, "The Cemetery as Cultural Institution: The Establishment of Mount Auburn and the 'Rural Cemetery' Movement". *American Quarterly* v. XXVI, no. 1, March, 1974, pp. 37-59. For a description of the same period of attitudinal change in England see James S. Curl, *The Victorian Celebration of Death,* Devon, David & Charles, 1972.

3 Thomas Haliburton, through the mouth of Sam Slick, the clockmaker, described St. Paul's graveyard, Halifax, in 1836. "You know where Governor Campbell lives, don't you, in a large stone house with a great wall round it, that looks like a state prison; well, near hand there is a nasty dirty horrid lookin' buryin' ground there — it's filled with large grave rats as big as kittens, and the springs of black water there, go through the chinks of the rocks and flow into all the wells, and fairly pyson the folks — it's a dismal place, I tell you . . . it's near about as nosey as a slave ship of niggers." (Haliburton, T.C. *The Clockmaker,* Boston, Benjamin B. Mussey, 1839, p. 87)

White Stone

1   Graves, Robert, *The White Goddess* (1948). New York, Noonday Press, 1969, p. 102.

2   You can distiguish calcite from dolomite, just by applying a drop or two of 10% hydrochloric acid to a fresh scratch on the stone. If it fizzes then it's calcite, if not, dolomite. Vinegar sometimes may be used but it is not always satisfactory. (Information from R. Grantham, Curator of Geology, Nova Scotia Museum.)

Flowers

1   Keese, John, ed., "The Language of Flowers". In *The Floral Keepsake*, N.Y., Leavitt and Allen, n.d. [c. 1850] pp. 101-111.

Masonic Imagery

1   The arch represents King Solomon's Temple; the central "G" means God or Deity (also Grandeur, Glory and Geometry); the three candlesticks are the three great lights in Masonry — the Holy Bible, square and compass. The square is emblematic of moral rectitude, the compass symbol of human reason and the key stresses the importance of Masonic Secrets; the anchor represents human hope; the ladder recalls Jacob's vision; the sun, moon and stars are symbolic of all nature's obedience to God; the eye is the All-Seeing Eye of God. There are many more. From Jean Lipman "An Early Masonic Meeting Place" *Antiques* vol. LV, no. 5, May 1949, pp. 355-7.

Cast Iron

1   One of the cast iron markers at Camp Hill Cemetery, Halifax, very similar to the plain Johns style, is marked "S.D." just to throw a spanner in the works, I'm sure.

2   Information from Stephen Archibald, Friend of Cast Iron Architecture.

White Bronze

1   Advertisement for W. H. Coffin, white bronze agent for Yarmouth, Shelburne and Queens Counties, in *Cape Sable Advertiser*, Barrington, N.S., Oct. 13, 1887.

Granite

1   Information supplied by Mr. Nelson of Heritage Memorials, D. W. Tingley of Tingley Monuments Ltd., and C. E. Dauphinee of W. T. Dauphinee Ltd., Dec. 1976.

Curiosities

1   King worked mainly in Halifax. He was involved in the construction of the Hobrecker (Oland) house on Young Ave. He also carved the Miner's Monument at Westville, Pictou Co., c. 1891. (Information from Mrs. S. W. Miller of Halifax, J. King's granddaughter.)

2   Family tradition has it that the monument was carved at F. A. Webster's request by S. F. Raymond of Yarmouth, who used a ceramic match holder of a woman standing by a sheaf of wheat for his model. The match holder is still in the possession of the Webster family. (Information from Miss Ellen Webster, Halifax, N.S.)

3   *Hants and Kings County Gazette*, May 5, 1834, vol. II, no. 27, p. 3.

4   Hart, John F. *History of North East Margaree*, n.p., Privately printed, 1963, p. 122.

The Hay Family of Halifax

1   Halifax Original Estate Papers, 1749-1842. P.A.N.S., C 19: Funeral Charges and Debts Laid by the Executors for the late Robert Campbell deceased. "July 30, 1776 To Cash paid James Hay for Gravestone £15.6.-."

2   *Nova Scotia Gazette and Weekly Chronicle*, Vol. X, no. 739, Aug. 1, 1780. p. 3, col. 1.

3   Punch, Terence M. "Assessment Rolls of Halifax, 1792 and 1793." *Genealogical Newsletter of the Nova Scotia Historical Society*, no. 11, April 1975, p. 18.

4   In late eighteenth century Halifax gravestone carving had not yet become a full time business, and mason's work really was more profitable.

5   Lewis Piers, Halifax merchant, left provision in his will (1779) for seven people, among them James Hay, to receive "tokens of Gratitude and Friendship" - the token being a "mourning Ring value one Guinea". At the same time he left "to John son to James Hay Five Guineas". Halifax Original Estate Papers, 1749-1842. P.A.N.S. proved March 2, 1779.

6 MacDonald, James S., *Annals of the North British Society, Halifax, N.S. 1768-1903.* Halifax, McAlpine Publishing Co. Ltd., 1905, p. 89.

7 Estate of Edmond Phelan, Halifax. "Paid Mr. John Hay for Gravestones£20.0.0., July 1st, 1803." Halifax Original Estate Papers, 1749-1842, P.A.N.S.

8 The Petition of John Hay of Halifax, Mason, May 17, 1820. P.A.N.S. Crown Land Grant Petitions.

9 Halifax Assessment Book 1817 #33; Halifax Assessment Book 1819. P.A.N.S.

10 Petition of John Hay, see footnote 8.

11 Halifax Original Estate Papers, 1749-1842. P.A.N.S., C 82: Estate of John Clewley "To Cash paid James Hay for a Head and Foot stone for the grave -£34-0-0".

12 *Nova Scotia Gazette and Weekly Chronicle* Vol. V, no. 257, June 13, 1775, p. 3, col. 1.

13 Grossman, Lloyd, "Heraldic Design on New England Gravestones" *Old Time New England* Vol. LXIV, no. 2., Oct-Dec 1973, pp. 55-60.

14 Ford, Paul Leicester, ed. *The New England Primer* (1897). N.Y., Teachers College, Columbia Univ., 1962, p. 27.

15 This stone was removed to the Nova Scotia Museum in July, 1977.

16 Halifax Assessment Rolls, 1817; 1819; 1821; 1822. P.A.N.S.

17 Peter Hay died in 1832 (*Nova Scotia Royal Gazette*, v. 31, no. 1635, May 30, 1832, p. 4, col. 3) He must have done the decorative carving and signed the stone, while the individual's information was added later by James Hay, his son, who continued his shop.

18 Halifax Original Estate Papers, 1842-1900, No. 57. P.A.N.S.

The Seaman Family of Horton and Cumberland

1 Gilroy, Marion, *Loyalists and Land Settlement in Nova Scotia,* Public Archives of Nova Scotia Publication No. 4, 1937, p. 41.

2 Eaton, A. W. H., *History of Kings County.* Salem, Mass., Salem Press, 1910, pp. 814-815.

3 Day Book of Timothy Bishop (1740-1827) covering 1775-1824, P.A.N.S. "Abraham Seaman moved to Pugwash November 22, 1821".

4 Kings County Probate Records, P.A.N.S. Estates of Timothy Barnaby, Cyrus Peck and Ezekiel Woodworth.

5 Observation by Mary Frederickson.

6 Estate of John Bishop, 1815. Kings County Probate Records, P.A.N.S. John Bishop was the uncle of Mercy Bishop, wife of Abraham Seaman.

7 This John Bishop was the grandfather of Mercy (Bishop) Seaman.

8 Estate of Dr. Jacob Walton, died April 28, 1840. Kings County Probate Records P.A.N.S. "Apr. 1, 1843, Cash paid Lewis Seaman balance due on acct. Gravestone."

9 *Hutchinson's N.S. Directory,* 1864-65. Halifax, R. T. Muir, 1864. p. 390.

10 *McAlpine's N.S. Directory,* 1866-67

11 *Lowell's N.S. Directory,* 1871. Interesting point: in 1871 T. L. Seaman was 74 years old.

J. W.

1 Since writing this I have discovered the Esther Sanford Stone (sandstone, 1822) at Scotch Village, Hants Co., which might be signed J.W. but is very worn. The lettering and sentiments are typical J.W. Although there are other J. W. stones dated before 1825, these appear to have been carved in his later period, and are probably backdated.

2 Vroom, F. W. *Memories of Windsor in the Seventies.* Windsor, N.S., Hants Journal, 1932, p. 9 (Personal copy of H. Piers, Nova Scotia Museum Printed Information Files.) Piers could have been wrong.

Bibliography

Primary Sources

Probate Records — Public Archives of Nova Scotia
Probate Records are kept in the Probate Office in each County seat.
Many of these are on microfilm at the PANS, but a great mass is
missing. The estate papers they have available are filed
alphabetically and/or chronologically, by county.

Newspapers and periodicals
I searched innumerable Nova Scotia newspapers and periodicals for
advertisements. This was not a systematic search, but rather as they
came to hand, I looked at them.

Individuals who supplied information:
Mr. C. E. Dauphinee, President of W. T. Dauphinee Ltd.,
Shelburne, N.S.
Dr. D. C. Mackay, Halifax, N.S.
Mr. Ross Graves, Genealogical Committee of the Nova Scotia
  Historical Society.
Dr. A. I. Ludwig, Montclair, New Jersey
Mrs. S. W. Miller, Halifax, N.S.
Mr. G. M. Nelson, Heritage Memorials Ltd., Windsor, N.S.
Mr. Willis Rice, Florida, formerly of Nictaux, Annapolis Co. N.S.
Mr. D. W. Tingley, Tingley Monuments Ltd., Amherst, Nova Scotia.

Directories

Hutchinson's Halifax Directory	1863
Hutchinson's Nova Scotia Directory	1864
Hutchinson's Nova Scotia Directory	1866
McAlpine's Nova Scotia Directory (2 Vol.)	1868
McAlpine's Halifax City Directory	1876
McAlpine's Halifax City Directory	1884
McAlpine's Halifax City Directory	1896
McAlpine's Halifax City Directory	1898
McAlpine's Directory of Nova Scotia	1914
McAlpine's Halifax City Directory	1918
McAlpine's Halifax City Directory	1922
McAlpine's Sydney City Directory	1923
McAlpine's Halifax City Directory	1927
Might's Halifax - Dartmouth City Directory	1936
Might's Halifax - Dartmouth City Directory	1937
Might's Halifax - Dartmouth City Directory	1938
Might's Halifax - Dartmouth City Directory	1940
Might's Halifax - Dartmouth City Directory	1944
Might's Halifax - Dartmouth City Directory	1947
Might's Halifax - Dartmouth City Directory	1949
Might's Halifax - Dartmouth City Directory	1950
Might's Halifax - Dartmouth City Directory	1952-1956
Might's Halifax - Dartmouth City Directory	1964
Might's Halifax - Dartmouth City Directory	1967-1968
Might's Halifax - Dartmouth City Directory	1970-1971
Might's Halifax - Dartmouth City Directory	1973
Might's Halifax - Dartmouth City Directory	1975
Teare's Directory of Pictou and New Glasgow	1879

Secondary Sources

Bender, Thomas
"The 'Rural' Cemetery Movement: Urban Travail and the Appeal of Nature" *New England Quarterly* v. XLVII, no. 2, June, 1974. pp. 196-211.
Burgess, Frederick
English Churchyard Memorials. London, Lutterworth Press, 1963.
Curl, James Stephen
The Victorian Celebration of Death. Devon, David & Charles, 1972

Deetz, James and
Edwin S. Dethlefsen
"Death's Head Cherub Urn and Willow". *Natural History* v. 76, no. 3, March 1967. pp. 28-37.
Dethlefsen, Edwin
and James Deetz.
"Death's Heads, Cherubs, and Willow Trees: Experimental Archaeology in Colonial Cemeteries". *American Antiquity* v. 31, no. 4, 1966. pp. 502-510.

French, Stanley
"The Cemetery as Cultural Institution: the Establishment of Mount Auburn and the 'Rural Cemetery' Movement". *American Quarterly* v. 26, no. 1. March 1974. pp. 37-59.
Forbes, Harriette Merrifield
Gravestones of Early New England and the Men Who Made Them 1653-1800. Boston, Houghton Mifflin, 1927. (New York, Da Capo Press, 1967)

Gillon, Edmund V.
Early New England Gravestone Rubbings. New York, Dover, 1966.
Gillon, Edmund V.
Victorian Cemetery Art. New York, Dover, 1972.

Hanks, Carol
Early Ontario Gravestones. Toronto, McGraw-Hill Ryerson, 1974.

Jacobs, G. Walker
Stranger Stop and Cast an Eye. Brattleboro, Vermont, Stephen Greene, 1972.

Ludwig, Allan I.
Graven Images: New England Stonecarving and its Symbols 1650-1815. Middletown, Conn., Wesleyan University Press, 1966.

Morse, William Inglis
Gravestones of Acadie. London, A. Smith & Co., 1929.
Morse, William Inglis
Land of New Adventure. London, Bernard Quaritch, 1932.
Mullane, George
A Monograph of Saint Paul's Cemetery. Halifax, John Burgoyne, 1902.

Perley, Sidney
"Early Gravestones in Essex County". *Essex Antiquarian* v. 3, no. 12, December, 1899. pp. 177-181.

Tashjian, Dickran
and Ann.
Memorials for Children of Change: The Art of Early New England Stonecarving. Middletown, Conn., Wesleyan University Press, 1974.

Wasserman, Emily
Gravestone Designs. New York, Dover, 1972.
Williams, Melvin G.
The Last Word. Boston, Oldstone Enterprises, 1973.
Wust, Klaus
Folk Art in Stone. Edinburg, Virginia, Shenandoah History, 1970.

142